You Can Get in the Way

How You Can Become a **ROADBLOCK** to Risk Factors

Dr. John W. Hodge

Duplication and Copyright

NCYI titles may be purchased in bulk at special discounts for educational, business, fundraising, or promotional use. For more information, please email sales@ncyi.org.

P.O. Box 22185 • Chattanooga, TN 37422-2185
423-899-5714 • 866-318-6294 • fax: 423-899-4547
www.ncyi.org

ISBN: 9781953945655
E-book: 9781953945662

A Library of Congress Control Number has been applied for and can be obtained from the Library of Congress.

© 2022 National Center for Youth Issues, Chattanooga, TN
All rights reserved.
Written by: Dr. John W. Hodge
Published by National Center for Youth Issues
Printed in U.S.A. • April 2022

To Mom, Dad, Mrs. Dawson, Thelma, and the many other angels in Heaven who continue to smile on me.

–John

Contents

See page 89 for information about Downloadable Resources.

Endorsements

This is the resource educators need! Short, actionable, and insightful, this book provides essential tools for teachers and encouragement for those in an industry that is often under-appreciated and under-resourced. At An Achievable Dream Academies, we implement these best practices and can testify to the success of the Roadblock Rules John shares. Drawing upon his extensive experience in education, John has created a tool that will encourage, inspire, and equip teachers everywhere to help their students overcome obstacles and achieve great things.

Lee Vreeland, Ed.D.
President & CEO, An Achievable Dream

I am currently a mental health therapist, but I started my journey as a classroom teacher. There are so many educators who simply need a boost today. In my opinion, this book is that boost. The ideas presented are powerful and practical regardless of the size of your school or the grade-level you teach. Thank you John for giving us strategies that really work.

Nikki Caldwell MS, LCMHC-S, CEO

I've been a teacher for almost 30-years, and was named Teacher-of-the-Year last year. Trust me, this is NOT the time for a huge book study. I'm exhausted! Teachers need a bite-sized reminder of the impact we can have on kids. Yes, I wanted to read this book. But I truly needed to read it. I felt inspired and validated. Well-done John!

Richelle Hodge
Middle School Teacher

I am currently a secondary mathematics coordinator and have known Dr. Hodge for 25 years. We have collaborated on countless projects and spent hours discussing the most effective ways to reach our most prized possessions. Children. I value our collaboration and shared vision that a positive, loving caring adult can change the trajectory of children and generations to come. He is not only the author of this positive publication, but his life's work is a testament of its contents! Ase' brother John!

James D. Hayden
Secondary Math Coordinator
Williamsburg-James City County Public Schools

---

*America's children are suffering from world and local events that are far beyond their control. Schools have been challenged in ways we've never experienced in public education. Many issues surrounding Covid 19 have become significant risk-factors for students, staffs and the communities that surround them. If not met with targeted interventions, the end-results of these risk-factors may still be apparent many years from now. Learning loss alone may impact future outcomes as today's elementary school students enter high school in the coming years. Practitioners must be concerned with much more than the achievement scores of students. Wellness and resilience must be a priority. Dr. Hodge has identified key "roadblocks" to risk-factors that will no doubt assist educators in providing needed support for students and colleagues. **John's timing is perfect.***

Richard A. Coleman, CFO
ULLC Inc.
Retired Principal

In my 50+ years as a public-school educator, I have worked as a teacher, building and district administrator, and as an educational consultant. In each of these roles I have tried to find resources to help me improve my craft, but all too often, my search has left me wanting. Many have addressed the technical skills of teaching without considering the relationship side. Others have offered insights into teacher-student relationships, but neglected the research-based strategies good teachers must utilize to help all students attain high academic achievement, especially those faced with intellectual and social/emotional barriers. Dr. Hodge offers an engaging and readable resource here for any teacher or administrator who wants to find the key to reach those kids who are not easy to teach and who do not respond to many traditional teaching practices. Many books simply give educators a "try harder" speech and a guilt trip for leaving these kids behind. Dr. Hodge offers hope and encouragement by providing a pathway to the promise. He gives us practical strategies which teachers and administrators can use today to remove the barriers which hinder so many students. This book is for educators who know we are called to equip all kids for much more than success in school---we are equipping them for life!

Dr. Harvey W. Perkins
CEO, Urban Learning and Leadership Center

To be in children's memories tomorrow, you have to be in their lives today.

Barbara Johnson

Introduction

I'm sitting in my office and the lights are purposefully dim. Urban Learning and Leadership Center (ULLC) is ending yet another successful year of business. Some might call this a miracle given the challenges we've faced. We've been helping schools to thrive for over twenty years, driven by our conviction that poverty and other risk factors need not be barriers to high student achievement. Children can be successful despite the risk factors that typically hold them back. All they need is for a few variables to operate in their favor. They need educators, counselors, social workers, community advocates, family members—people just like you— who can see beyond poverty and other limitations to the *unlimited* potential that lies within the hearts and minds of all children.

> *They need educators, counselors, social workers, community advocates, family members—people just like you—who can see beyond poverty and other limitations to the **unlimited** potential that lies within the hearts and minds of all children.*

The evidence is overwhelming that one person's willingness to act can enhance resilience in children to such an extent that they overcome obstacles and eventually thrive. And I believe that one person just might be *you*.

This book will clearly explain how the actions of caring adults have been the difference between success and failure for children like the ones you see in your schools every day. As you read, you will gain a fundamental understanding of how the resilience phenomenon works and gain insight into ways you may be able to foster resilience in students. Put simply, we must enhance resilience in students by *getting in the way* of the risk factors that may hold them back. By doing this, we increase their likelihood of achieving success.

Within the context of this book, "getting in the way" means forming a barrier and literally becoming a roadblock between children and the risk factors that too often make failure more likely for large numbers of kids. Your ability to get in the way is not dependent on where you teach, the age of your students, or the number of years you have worked with young people. Getting in the way is often more about *will* than *skill*.

Let me be perfectly honest: I almost didn't write this book. There were funerals, lost jobs, lost homes, lost revenue, and lost hope in many of our communities. But when I step back and really think about it, challenges like these take place every year of our lives. Even if you're reading this book in the year 2032, I'll bet you agree! The truth is, I've been alive for over half a century, and there has not been a single year of my life during which tragedies have not taken place. I worked with schools in Louisiana after Hurricane Katrina. I've worked with children who have lost their parents to war. My wife and I have both lost students to gang violence. Pick almost any year in almost any location, and you'll find that tragic events have impacted families. As I type these words, I don't know what the future holds. Nobody does! But here is a fact that is indisputable for those of us in the field of education: our collective ability to enhance resilience will remain absolutely necessary for the success of our students right now and into the future—period, full stop.

> *...our collective ability to enhance resilience will remain absolutely necessary for the success of our students right now and into the future...*

We may have challenging days ahead, but I am completely convinced that our resilience can get us through whatever obstacles we face. Resilience is an element of social-emotional wellness that is applicable to students and staff in all schools. With that in mind, I hope this book educates and motivates you in your efforts to be the difference in the lives of your students in elementary school, middle school, high school, and beyond. Please know that the journey to success for many students starts with you. If you truly want to enhance resilience in others, start by acknowledging your own. We are all much stronger than we think. You have overcome obstacles to arrive where you are. Remind yourself of this fact as often as you can.

As you read through the following motivational stories and gain practical strategies to *get in the way* of the strengths and weaknesses that prevent students from reaching their highest potential, you may need to acknowledge your own risk factors in order to maximize your effectiveness as an educator. I fundamentally believe there is something profoundly great within you that, when leveraged, can help you elevate greatness in yourself and others, including kids in your classroom, individuals in your caseload, colleagues, leaders in your school district, parents, and even community stakeholders whose tax dollars support public schools. There is a miracle waiting to happen in you and through you for those around you.

I have been a national consultant for many years. I have worked with over three hundred school districts that served over one million students in the United States, Canada, and South America. In the thousands of miles I've traveled, I've often been inspired by the stories shared with me in schools all over North America. I've kept a journal of inspiring individuals and saved their heroic efforts for a time in my life when I would finally be able to share just a few of them in a book. That time is right now.

The stories in this book were carefully changed to maintain anonymity and protect the privacy of those who inspired them. The caring adults featured are my greatest heroes for one simple reason: they cared enough to act. By reading their stories, I hope you are inspired to do the same. Before we get to specific stories, we will begin our journey in Chapter 1 with a brief discussion of the history of school accountability and explain why resilience is relevant in today's schools.

The Reality of School Accountability:
Why Resilience Is Relevant

Do you work in an accredited school? Have your students met or exceeded the academic standards of your state? These are common topics today. But those of you who are seasoned educators may recall a time in our profession when end-of-year state assessments did not exist. We didn't talk about state tests or accreditation. If a school had great teams, a good music program, happy kids, and happy parents, it was usually considered a *good* school by members of the community. I know this may sound strange to many of you reading this, but the academic achievement of our most vulnerable students was rarely reported a few decades ago.

In 1989, an education summit held by the National Governors' Association resulted in a national commitment to develop academic standards for each core subject area. These standards were developed to clearly articulate what students should know and be able to do at each grade level. Legislation in the 1990s called Goals 2000 required states to create and assess academic standards in core subject areas. Other than integration, this may have been the most significant legislation targeting education in the last hundred years. The assessment requirement gave birth to the end-of-year testing that became the norm.

In the late 1990s, I was a very young administrator in an affluent middle school. Let me give you just one example of what I mean when I say "affluent." The most popular orthodontist sent *limousines* to pick up our students for their appointments. Get the picture? The National Blue Ribbon Schools Program recognized our school for excellence. Though we were considered a great school, we were never *really* held accountable for the achievement levels of our minority or low-income students. Other than student advocates, no one ever inquired about the academic success of our students with special needs. State testing and accountability hit schools in my district like a ton of bricks in the late nineties. Academic achievement became an integral part of public discourse. The achievement levels of schools were front-page news in our community. When this began to happen, the last place an educator wanted to be was in a *failing* school.

As fate would have it, I was assigned to a failing school in 1999. Within three years, we were able to turn the school around, and our success gained the positive attention of our state's department of education. This attention was fueled by the No Child Left Behind Act of 2001. Three colleagues and I formed an organization called Urban Learning and Leadership Center, and our journey of helping other struggling schools began.

In the fall of 2002, Dr. Jo Lynne DeMary, superintendent of public instruction for the Virginia Department of Education, requested that the Urban Learning and Leadership Center provide training for schools listed in Governor Mark Warner's Partnership for Achieving Successful Schools (PASS) initiative. PASS targeted more than one hundred academically warned schools based on the results of the state's most recent end-of-year exams. Every year, hundreds of thousands of kids in the Commonwealth of Virginia take state assessments, called SOL tests. And no, I am not making up the name. We really do call them SOL tests. Among several other possible interpretations that may be going through your mind as you smile right now, SOL stands for Standards of Learning.

Like all other states, Virginia has academic standards for K–12 accreditation. This remains the reality of public schools in America today. At the beginning of the PASS initiative, thirty-four of the targeted PASS schools were specifically designated as *priority schools* due to their low performance on state assessments and were strongly encouraged to attend a conference called the Governor's Urban Learning and Leadership Institute. In my capacity as a founder of Urban Learning and Leadership Center, I was part of the planning, development, and delivery of content for the conference. Keep in mind that schools encouraged to attend events like this are often labeled in the media as failing schools, comprehensive schools, targeted schools, and so on. Some states bypass the labels and simply give A through F grades to schools. This well-intentioned attempt to hold schools accountable overlooked the reality that labeling a school also labels the kids and adults in it. For this very reason, part of my job involves simply motivating students and staff.

Regardless of the state, failing labels or grades are tough pills to swallow for those who work tirelessly in these schools every day. Don't get me wrong, the public has a right to know the performance levels of publicly funded schools. But I remember how it felt to work in a school with a negative label. The stress of such labels can negatively impact the morale of students and staff if not countered with a firm commitment to achieve excellence. I can clearly remember students saying things like, "We go to a failing school. That means we're stupid."

As you might imagine, educators who attended the Governor's Institute were not exactly happy to be there. Some in attendance even joked that Governor Warner gave teachers a GIFT: Governor's Institute for Failing Teachers. I can vividly remember a comment made by a somewhat disgruntled participant at one of our training sessions. After expressing resentment that his school was "labeled" a failing school, he then commented, "These children can't be successful because the deck is stacked against them." As long as I live, I will never forget these words, mainly because I've heard versions of this same statement across the United States in the years since I first heard them. I cannot discount the fact that circumstances can make academic success more difficult. The good news is that although the deck is, in fact, stacked against millions of America's children, success it still achievable. This is why resilience is relevant in America's schools.

In a groundbreaking study of the resilience phenomenon, Emmy E. Werner and Ruth S. Smith traced the lives of a cohort of children from birth into adulthood.[1] Most of the parents of children who participated in the study had limited education. Participating children endured a variety of other circumstances that placed them at risk of social failure. Through case studies and the statistical analysis of multiple variables, Werner and Smith found that many of the children were able to overcome life's challenges and become caring, productive adults.

As early investigators of resilience, the research of Werner and Smith was foundational and helped to clarify key differences between children who successfully navigate adverse circumstances and those who do not. More importantly for the purposes of our discussion, their research clearly established the fact that children can be successful regardless of adverse circumstances. In keeping with the card metaphor mentioned previously, the problem is not that the deck is stacked against children. In many cases, the problem is that the adults who work with them place too much emphasis on the wrong cards in the deck. In other words, they focus too much of their attention on a child's deficits rather than their assets. The research of Drs. Steve and Sybil Wolin asserts that those who foster resilience in children are able to recognize a child's strengths despite the presence of obvious challenges.[2]

Listen, I have been there. I know what it's like to feel overwhelmed by circumstances and challenges beyond our control that impact children in our schools each day. I also know that it is easy to become so consumed by these circumstances and challenges that you become blind to the possibility that kids can overcome obstacles. An understanding of resilience can help educators and other practitioners to see beyond circumstances and embrace the possibility of success. In my many years in education, I have found that we often get what we expect from children. When the adults who work with children embrace the realization that success is possible despite adversity, high levels of achievement are more likely to occur.

Education Policy and the Achievement Gap

With so much emphasis on test scores in many of our schools, I feel that it's important to briefly discuss the policies that helped create our current reality. I promise not to venture too far down the policy rabbit hole. However, a brief discussion will enhance your understanding of the relevance of resilience in our efforts to help students achieve academic goals. Those of us who analyze achievement data clearly see that students with certain risk factors struggle to reach desired achievement levels.

Nationally, schools have struggled with a very clear and consistent achievement gap in many urban, suburban, and rural areas. This gap became more glaring after the implementation of the No Child Left Behind Act, which was signed into law on January 8, 2001. No Child Left Behind was the first time in the history of public schools in the United States that school success was measured by the achievement levels of traditionally underserved and underperforming student populations. Under the law, assessment results were categorized and disaggregated according to socioeconomic status, disability, race, and limited English proficiency.

Those who supported the policy believed that it marked the first time in the history of public education that *every child mattered— really mattered*—due to the new wave of accountability. This legislation made sweeping changes to the role of the federal government in educating children and was specifically designed to help close the achievement gap between disadvantaged students and their more affluent, less challenged peers.

Today's academic standards are even more rigorous, and new federal guidelines continue to hold school districts accountable for the performance of children who are forced to contend with challenges far beyond their control, such as poverty. Those of us who are in the trenches know that the enhanced rigor of state standards and the persistence of challenges that accompany poverty make high academic achievement more difficult. The Every Student Succeeds Act was introduced and signed into law on December 10, 2015. Funding for this law was authorized to last through 2021. The purpose of ESSA was to update No Child Left Behind and continue to hold schools accountable for the success of *all* students.

It is inevitable that newer versions of previous public policies will continue to impact classrooms and schools directly in the foreseeable future. For the individual teacher, these policies mean that the performance of your students will continue to be measured and directly impact the rating of your school. This also means that academic standards for success may become more difficult to achieve. In America's schools, high academic achievement will likely remain our primary goal, regardless of our subject areas or grade levels. In order to reach these higher levels of achievement, we must adopt strategies that help students to fight through adverse circumstances. We cannot discount the harsh reality that the challenges our students face make high academic achievement more difficult to attain. The fundamental connection between student success and resilience is the fact that challenges need not be barriers to success.[3] This connection makes an understanding of resilience imperative for those of us who work with America's children. Resilience is relevant and important!

You Can Get In the Way   How You Can Become a ROADBLOCK to Risk Factors

The Basics of Resilience:

Now that We Know It's Important, What Exactly Is It?

In the first chapter, we discussed school accountability and the relevance of resilience in our efforts to meet state accreditation standards. Let's continue our journey with a practical, plain-language definition of resilience that will guide our discussion for the rest of the book. *Resilience* refers to the ability to avoid, bypass, navigate, bounce back from, get through, get over, go around, or survive adversities of all kinds. It's easy to find a plethora of research and commentary on resilience. Researchers and practitioners debate different types of traits that are sometimes referred to as *resiliencies*. There is also a degree of debate among scholars as to whether resilience refers to a set of skills, a process, or simply a desired end result.

While aspects of the resilience phenomenon may be debatable, what's most important to those of us who currently work with students is the fact that the resilience of students can be enhanced due to the actions of caring adults. In other words, the actions of caring adults can help students to overcome adversity. With the right support, resilience can be developed in the students with whom we work. This opens the door to two phenomenal realities:

1. Your actions can impact a child in such a way that the impact of adversity is reduced.
2. You can directly teach a child to overcome adversity.

Just typing these words makes me excited and optimistic about the future.

Resilience literature is expansive. While studying the phenomenon on the campus of Virginia Tech, my first immersion into the topic led me to the field of medicine and the impact of resilience on health and recovery. Further investigation became almost overwhelming. Resilience is an important consideration in many fields of study. According to the United States Department of Energy, resilience encompasses over forty different definitions in a variety of academic disciplines including engineering, education, and psychology. After studying the topic for almost twenty years, I've decided to let others debate its idiosyncrasies. For the purposes of this book, I'll direct our focus on the resilience phenomenon as it pertains to the challenges we face in America's schools. While I am extremely interested in its proven applicability to better outcomes in health, I must stay focused. To do otherwise would turn this shorter book into five hundred pages. And who among us has time for that between teaching, testing, grades, parent meetings, PLCs, grade-level meetings, department meetings, contact tracing, webinars, and so on?

Whether rich or poor, young or old, black or white, we are shaped by our experiences. Some of us have been fortunate enough to live without the emotional stressors that plague many citizens. Others struggle daily, from the moment they wake until the moment they go to sleep. This is clearly articulated in the research of Werner and Smith. Resilience literature gives us what some believe is a more comprehensive vantage point from which to consider life and its events. Bad stuff happens to people. Success or failure depends on how people react to bad stuff. This is probably oversimplified, but I'm sure you understand my meaning.

To me, Emmy Werner and Ruth Smith are superheroes of the resilience phenomenon. Their research followed a cohort of children for multiple decades and opened the door for the research that followed. While I never met these scholars, their research literally saved my dissertation, which started with a fundamental question: "What makes success more likely for kids deemed unlikely to be successful?" Those of you in or beyond grad school probably realize that this was a poorly constructed question. Trust me, one of my Virginia Tech professors critiqued it vigorously. But he continuously encouraged my pursuit of the answer. The success and/or failure of today's kids often depends on the interaction between their assets and liabilities. In resilience literature, assets and liabilities are called protective factors and risk factors.

Risk Factors vs. Protective Factors

Risk factors and protective factors remain in dynamic interplay. They consistently clash and interact within the context of daily life. For the educator, counselor, social worker, or mentor, this dynamic interplay offers hope that the risk factors in a child's life need not doom that child to failure. The compelling work of Steve and Sybil Wolin suggest that when you get in the way, when you become a roadblock to risk factors, you become a protective factor that makes success more likely for kids.[4] For example, when educators help students avoid the risk of poor attendance by enthusiastically welcoming children into the school daily, they are functioning as protective factors for the children they serve. A well-placed, consistent protective factor—like a committed educator—can mitigate the impact of some of the most challenging risk factors in a child's life.

Risk factors are a part of daily life and are embedded within every facet of our existence.

Put simply, risk factors tend to make life more difficult in a variety of ways. Consider the life of Elise, who is ten years old. Elise was born to a single mother in one of America's most violent neighborhoods, surrounded by some of her state's lowest-performing schools. Her mom works two jobs and barely makes ends meet financially. Nutritional options are limited to foods high in sugar that fall far short of the recommended daily allowance of vitamins and minerals needed for healthy physical and cognitive growth. Elise has trouble attending school and rarely completes homework assignments. When she does attend, she typically arrives late and misses the school's breakfast program. Despite many extracurricular activities, Elise most often leaves school immediately after the final bell and misses evening meals provided by the school.

Elise's life is marked by a typical collection of inescapable risk factors that exist in the lives of millions of America's children. In order to make success more likely for Elise, practitioners must ask a fundamental question: What school programs can be leveraged to mitigate risk factors and make success more likely for Elise and others like her?

Think about our definition of *resilience*. Think about the resources that are available to Elise. What could assist her to avoid, navigate, bounce back from, get through, get over, go around, or survive the adversities present in her life? For kids lucky enough to have a caring adult who is willing to undertake this type of analysis, success is much more likely. Take a moment to make a list of the risk factors present in Elise's life. Then list the resources that may help to mitigate the risks. Simple processes like this can spark discussions that lead to solutions that help children like Elise to overcome barriers to success.

["RISK FACTORS IN THE LIFE OF ELISE"]

RISK FACTORS	RESOURCES

With the right support, little girls like Elise can become successful adults. I've seen it happen with my own eyes at a school called An Achievable Dream (AAD) Academy in Newport News, Virginia. At the time, An Achievable Dream Academy was located in one of the city's most crime-infested areas. During my tenure, the academy was a K–8 public school. Approximately 97 percent of its students met the criteria for free or reduced-price lunch. And over 85 percent of students came from single-parent homes. The educators in this building put to rest any doubt about a child's ability to thrive despite risk factors. And today, over twenty years later, they have expanded their efforts to include three additional school districts and five campuses collectively serving pre-kindergarten through twelfth-grade students.

The foundational philosophy of the school remains grounded in research. It is a shared philosophy that bears repeating often: the risk factors associated with poverty need not be barriers to academic success if the right support structures are put into place. The good news is that you don't have to be a teacher at this amazing school to apply this philosophy. Allow me to share what An Achievable Dream was able to accomplish. This short list that follows was compiled in 2009 by Dr. Lee Vreeland, current president and chief executive officer of An Achievable Dream. Under her leadership, the program has reached more students and even higher levels of success.

- From 2001 to 2009, AAD maintained a 99 percent on-time graduation rate.
- Eighty-two percent of all AAD graduates are confirmed to be enrolled in college, the military, a trade school, or gainfully employed.
- AAD had the highest eighth-grade writing scores in Newport News with a pass rate of 96 percent.
- AAD has the highest eighth-grade social studies scores in Newport News with a pass rate of 91 percent.
- An Achievable Dream Academy and An Achievable Dream Middle and High School are both fully accredited and made Adequate Yearly Progress.

Today, An Achievable Dream Academies leverage the power of community stakeholders and influencers to alleviate the impact of risk for hundreds of students in Virginia. An Achievable Dream has been in existence for decades, and the harsh reality is that many of us don't have the benefit of this level of systemic support. But don't be discouraged!

Individuals Can Have an Impact

My friend Terry Greenlund became so frustrated fighting against the impact of risk factors that he convinced families to send their children to boarding schools with funding donated by Terry and others. This is a novel idea that's been extremely effective for the children who have participated. But this strategy is not feasible to the masses. Thankfully, one caring adult may be able to replicate similar results with efforts in traditional schools. According to a paper by the National Scientific Council on the Developing Child in collaboration with Harvard's Jack Shonkoff, a strong relationship with one adult is key to helping students to develop successful responses to significant adversity.[5] These relationships have a measurable effect on student outcomes.

John Hattie is perhaps the most quoted educational researcher in the area of effect size. Well, what is effect size? Put in simple terms, effect size simply means impact. It is used to measure the impact of policies, procedures, and programs in the field of education and other disciplines. Ranges are used to highlight and describe varying effects. The following table can be used to aid your analysis of effect size.

Effect Size Ranges	Description of Impact
0.00–0.20	Statistically significant but barely noteworthy; very small or unclear impact
0.20–0.40	Small to moderate impact; generally below desired impact
0.40–0.60	Very strong effects; noteworthy; desirable
0.60–2.00	Extreme impact!

Further investigation of Hattie's work offers hopeful news for schools forced to deal with circumstances beyond their control due to the economic disadvantages endured by their students.[6] Schools cannot control risk factors that may be based on where students live, the income of parents, or the level of violence in neighborhoods. However, factors that are within the locus of control of schools can be leveraged for noteworthy effects on student achievement. What's even more encouraging is that the strategies listed in the table below can be implemented by individual teachers to achieve powerful results.

Element/Strategy	Effect Size/Impact	Locus of Control
Feedback	1.13	School/Classroom/Staff
Instructional Quality	1.00	School/Classroom/Staff
Direct Instruction	.82	School/Classroom/Staff

We should all be encouraged by this research. Let me be clear: children are impacted by risk factors that are beyond our control. Consider the various challenges endured by Elise. However, there are strategies, processes, and procedures that have been shown to have an extremely positive impact on student achievement, despite the presence of risk. And many of these factors are directly within the locus of control of individuals just like you. If we control the variables that are within our sphere of influence, many of the risk factors that negatively impact student achievement can be overcome. By simply controlling what is within our control, we can essentially get in the way of risks. As stated in my preface, getting in the way is often a matter of will, not skill. That being said, we must strongly consider which actions we are willing to take in order for our students to be successful.

James Hayden and the Power of Relationships

James Hayden is one of the most accomplished teachers I have ever met. In our area of Virginia, many of us know him as Super Teacher. And trust me, the moniker fits perfectly. I have known

James for well over twenty-five years. When I was assigned by my district to go to An Achievable Dream Academy, James was the very first teacher I recruited to join me.

James has mastered the instructional strategies required for success in a high-poverty classroom. During his many years as a teacher, his daily learning targets, lesson plans, and formative assessments were carefully aligned with the state's rigorous standards. He used technology and a variety of teaching methodologies to keep his students engaged, and he checked for understanding on an ongoing basis to see where learning gaps existed. Knowing the standards and being skillful at the art and science of teaching are essential in our quest for high academic achievement. But students with multiple risk factors often require more than instructional proficiency on the part of their teacher. **They need a true connection.**

During my years as a district-level administrator, I was a part of a strategic effort to increase the number of minority students in honors and AP classes. At the time, there were fewer than five African American students taking calculus in the entire district. This was staggering considering the fact that our district served approximately thirty thousand students, most of whom were African American. The pathway to calculus in high school begins in elementary and middle school. A key indicator that a student has made adequate progress toward advanced mathematics in high school is success in algebra and geometry at the middle school level.

In 1997 James Hayden invited me to visit his middle school algebra class at a high-performing middle school in our district. At the time, algebra and geometry classes at the middle school level in our district were typically filled with students designated as *gifted*. And most of them were white and affluent. When I visited

Mr. Hayden's class, I was embarrassingly shocked to discover that twenty-five of his twenty-eight seventh graders in algebra were African American. I admit my embarrassment in order to illustrate the fact that *we all must challenge our expectations*. Remember, we get what we expect.

One of the keys to Mr. Hayden's success with students was his ability to develop healthy relationships with all students, regardless of their risk factors. His ability to do this is so noteworthy that I actually mentioned Mr. Hayden in my dissertation on resilience. He was able to help students achieve success in rigorous math courses by connecting with kids in meaningful ways. In other words, the development of relationships was essential pedagogy.

Children who are most vulnerable to risk factors often find it much easier to learn from teachers with whom they have a positive bond. This may sound oversimplified, but it is impossible for me to overstate the following reality for educational practitioners: many students don't care how much adults *know* until they know how much adults *care*. Mr. Hayden, the Super Teacher, realized that he did not teach a subject. *He taught children*. His kids were more important to him than his subject area. They were more important to him than state test scores, and they knew it. He showed them by meeting kids who needed extra help before and after school, calling parents with good news, talking to kids about their interests beyond school, and showing patience in the face of behavioral challenges. Mr. Hayden showed his students that he really cared, and phenomenal test results followed. The fact that over 90 percent of his African American, middle school students passed high school algebra and geometry *while in middle school* is proof of the power of relationships. When healthy relationships with caring adults are established, children begin to exhibit behaviors that are consistent with resilience:

1. **They show up to class on time.**
2. **They come to school prepared.**
3. **They put forth more effort toward the completion of assignments.**
4. **They behave in ways that produce academic success in elementary, middle, and high school.**
5. **They surround themselves with positive peers and adults.**
6. **They make productive daily decisions.**
7. **They avoid and/or bounce back from challenges.**[7]

Now pause and think about the behavioral outcomes previously listed. Students who consistently demonstrate these behaviors are considered resilient. What is a student's trajectory in life who demonstrates these behaviors on a regular basis? Careful consideration of this fundamental question will help you see the importance of resilience more clearly.

In the many notes of my dissertation research, the perception on the part of resilient children that their teachers really cared for them emerged as an important theme. All interview participants clearly indicated that caring adults were essential to helping them overcome the daily challenges they faced. Think about children like Elise—a caring adult can become a roadblock to risk factors by motivating them to put forth more effort, show up to school on time, and take classroom lessons seriously. When kids do this, they soon discover that they can be successful regardless of the risk factors all around them. In a study of inner-city youth in Denver, the ability to achieve favorable outcomes despite significant neighborhood risk factors was deemed more likely when positive bonds between students and teachers were present.[8]

Based on the information we have covered in Chapters 1 and 2, now would be a great time to begin an ongoing list of strategies that can be used by any educator, at any grade level, in any district to foster resilience. What shall we call this list? Let's keep it super simple: Roadblock Rules (R^2). These rules will be followed by sections called Implementation Imperatives. These imperatives will offer you practical ideas on how to make the rules come alive in your classrooms and schools. In the chapters that follow, this list will synthesize information into recommendations and reminders that can be implemented individually or shared with colleagues in learning communities for systemic success. Although the list is primarily written for teachers, it is applicable to all of us who work with students, including counselors, social workers, and other staff members. Chapter 3 was written to emphasize the fact that you don't have to be a licensed practitioner to protect students from risk factors. In many cases, all that is required is a willingness to act.

Roadblock Rules (R^2)

1.	Utilize effective instructional practices.
2.	Establish positive relationships with students that demonstrate genuine care and concern.

Implementation Imperatives: Rule #1—Effective Instructional Practices

The prospect of using effective instructional practices gives us much to consider. Most school districts have specifically outlined what they regard as effective practice. ULLC uses several indicators to assess instructional practices, including the following key elements. This may help create a process for your school if you don't have one in place currently.

Key Elements of Effective Instruction

1. INSTRUCTIONAL OBJECTIVE
(Scored as observed "Yes" or "No" with comments)

   a. Is a written objective / learning target clearly visible?
   Yes _____ No _____
   Comments: _____
   _____

   b. Does it articulate in student-friendly terms what the student is to know or be able to do at the end of that daily lesson?
   Yes _____ No _____
   Comments: _____
   _____

   c. Does it address what the student is to learn as opposed to describing an activity?
   Yes _____ No _____
   Comments: _____
   _____

2. SUPPORTIVE INSTRUCTIONAL ENVIRONMENT
(Scored as observed "Yes" or "No" with comments).

   a. Are the majority of the students exhibiting attentive, responsive behaviors?
   Yes _____ No _____
   Comments: _____
   _____

   b. Was there a sense of calm and mutual respect between students and the teacher?
   Yes _____ No _____
   Comments: _____
   _____

   c. Did the behaviors of students interfere with the delivery of the lesson?
   Yes _____ No _____
   Comments: _____
   _____

3. STUDENT ENGAGEMENT
(Scored as observed "Yes" or "No" with comments).

a. Were 50 percent or more of the students intentionally focused on an instructional activity linked to the daily lesson objective?

Yes _____ No _____

Comments: _____

_____

b. Were the following types of engagement evident: students paying attention, taking notes, asking focused questions, responding to questions, and reacting with interest as they pursued the learning target? Off-task behaviors yielding a negative response include students misbehaving, heads on desks, having off-topic discussions, or causing disruptions. Off-task behaviors also include students doing assigned tasks without a clear connection to the learning target. Copying from the board or playing unfocused instructional games/software activities are examples.

Yes _____ No _____

Comments: _____

_____

4. CHECKING FOR UNDERSTANDING
(Scored as observed "Yes" or "No" with comments).

a. Does the teacher use a variety of techniques throughout the lesson to determine if all of the students are mastering the content as it is being taught?

Yes _____ No _____

Comments: _____

_____

b. Does the teacher use effective strategies to keep a pulse on the mastery level of all students throughout the teaching process (flash cards, white boards, walkabouts, exit cards, signaling, etc.)? Calling on students whose hands are raised first, single student responses, callouts, and general choral responses are not positive indicators.

Yes _____ No _____

Comments: _____

_____

5. ACADEMIC RIGOR

(Scored as a percentage of observed/heard written or oral questions in presentations or assessments at various levels of Webb's Depth of Knowledge [DOK] model).

a. Does the teacher scaffold oral questions and written questions in classwork, assigned tasks, and assessments to go beyond DOK levels 1 and 2 to include higher-order thinking at levels 3 and 4?

- Level 1: Recall and Reproduction: Tasks at this level require recall of facts or rote application of simple procedures. The task does not require any cognitive effort beyond remembering the right response or formula. Copying, computing, defining, and recognizing are typical Level 1 tasks.

- Level 2: Skills and Concepts: At this level, a student must make some decisions about their approach. Tasks with one or more mental steps, such as comparing, organizing,summarizing, predicting, and estimating are usually Level 2.

- Level 3: Strategic Thinking: At this level of complexity, students must use planning and evidence. The thinking at this level is more abstract. A task with multiple valid responses where students must justify their choices would be Level 3. Examples include solving nonroutine problems, designing an experiment, or analyzing characteristics of a genre.

- Level 4: Extended Thinking: These tasks require the most complex cognitive effort. Students synthesize information from multiple sources, often over an extended period of time, or transfer knowledge from one area of focus to solve problems in another. Designing a survey and interpreting the results, analyzing multiple texts to extract themes, or writing an original myth in an ancient style would all be examples of Level 4.

The elements listed in the charts above are just a few of the many considerations one must ponder when attempting to use effective instructional practices.

Implementation Imperatives: Rule #2—Relationships

It is virtually impossible to overstate the importance of relationships with students. Children tend to learn more from teachers with whom they share healthy relationships. Kindness is essential to building the foundation to good relationships with kids. Consistent kindness builds the kind of trust that students often remember long after they've left the school. Be clear about what you expect and overtly model the behaviors you desire. Praise kids for doing the right thing. And when we correct negative behaviors, we should do it in ways that show children that we dislike their behavior but care about them as people. Simple tools like interest inventories and/or unofficial interviews can help adults gain important insights that help kids become more passionate about learning and make success more likely.

//////////////// ◇ 3 ◇ ////////////////

How Ordinary People Got in the Way for Kids Like Me

Donald Humphrey was an elementary school custodian and avid basketball fan. He grew up in the community in which he worked and knew many of the kids and their families. In the early to mid-eighties, the crack cocaine epidemic gripped urban America like a vise. And our government's response made the situation even worse for many communities.

Citizens were told to "Just Say No" to one of the most addictive drugs in human history.[9] For those who lacked the willpower to follow this advice, mass incarceration was the solution. In Donald's case, the rapid deterioration of his neighborhood understandably had a negative impact on kids. This phenomenon was not limited to just one city or state. The crack epidemic impacted the entire country without warning and turned relatively good neighborhoods into war zones from California to North Carolina. The number of crack cocaine users increased by 1.6 million people between 1982 and 1985.[10] Like the more recent opioid crisis, communities were devastated. The violence that resulted from the distribution, sale, and use of drugs obliterated safe havens like community parks in many neighborhoods. And our most vulnerable population, our children, suffered most.

The impact on children went beyond just living in danger. Many lost their parents who became hopelessly addicted to a drug for which adequate treatment centers were never established. The logical outgrowth of these desperate community conditions was significant. The changes in student outcomes clearly showed a decline in measures of achievement, particularly for African American males. The impact of crack cocaine is estimated to account for approximately 40 to 70 percent of the fall in black male high school graduation rates.[11] It is with these conditions as a societal backdrop that a man named Donald Humphrey got in the way. His actions show us that supporting resilience in children often begins with a willingness to act on the part of an adult.

Some might call Donald insignificant because of his job title. My observations of how the resilience phenomenon functions make it abundantly clear that helping kids become more resilient has little to do with job titles and more to do with action. Others might have considered Donald powerless. He had no wealth. His level of education was limited. His influence on school or district policy was slim to none. But Donald Humphrey had two extremely important assets needed to buffer the impact of neighborhood risk factors like violence and unsupervised children:

1. Donald had a willingness to help.
2. Donald had the keys to the school's gymnasium.

And with these two assets, Donald got in the way of potentially harmful circumstances that could have damaged the lives of the kids with whom he worked.

What he did was rather simple and some would say accidental. Donald transformed the lives of children in ways that are difficult to completely quantify. We can measure improvements in attendance and academic performance. It's far more challenging to quantitatively capture what it means to a nine-year-old that he has a safe place to be after school. That is what Donald provided.

It all started with a conversation in the assistant principal's office. We all know the vicious cycle of discipline referrals that takes place in thousands of schools across the country. We also know that the academic achievement of a child is rarely improved by sitting in the assistant principal's office. Yet thousands of kids are sent to these offices every day where they continue to fall behind academically as they wait for punishment. You know the cycle:

We also know that the academic achievement of a child is rarely improved by sitting in the assistant principal's office.

This is the cycle that leads to academic failure, unemployment, and prison for kids across the United States.

On one particular day, Donald was emptying a trash can in the assistant principal's office when Jamal Patterson was referred for a second time that day. Donald normally kept quiet while he was doing his job in the office. But today was different. You see, Donald knew Jamal. They lived in the same neighborhood and, on occasion, even attended the same church. Donald knew Jamal's entire family: mom, dad, uncles, aunts, and grandparents. When Jamal arrived in the office, the assistant principal noticed the look of shock and embarrassment when Jamal saw Donald. Before even acknowledging the assistant principal, Jamal's eyes gazed up at Donald's six-foot, six-inch frame—a frame that had fallen just short of a college basketball scholarship many years ago.

Chart Circle

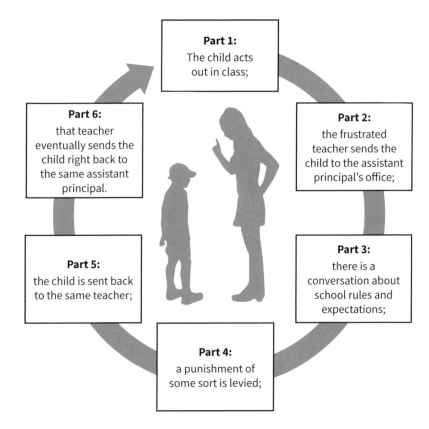

Part 1:
The child acts out in class;

Part 2:
the frustrated teacher sends the child to the assistant principal's office;

Part 3:
there is a conversation about school rules and expectations;

Part 4:
a punishment of some sort is levied;

Part 5:
the child is sent back to the same teacher;

Part 6:
that teacher eventually sends the child right back to the same assistant principal.

Jamal spoke barely above a whisper, "Hey, Mr. Donald."

Donald replied, "What's up little man? I know you're not in trouble?"

Without saying a word, Jamal slowly handed the dreaded office discipline referral to the assistant principal, who immediately said to Donald, "This is the second time I've seen Jamal today."

Jamal didn't seem to care much about the normal punitive actions of his assistant principal. But he could barely look Donald in the eyes at that moment. This is where a small resilience miracle began because Donald decided to get in the way of the risk factors. And please be mindful and encouraged that what I am about to explain to you could happen in any school in any state. Again, it starts with a willingness to act.

Donald said to the assistant principal, "I know Jamal's family. Instead of in-school suspension, why don't you let Jamal stay after school with me? He can help me clean up the place. Trust me, his folks won't mind."

The assistant principal replied, "That might be a good idea. Let me check with his mom and get back to you."

When the assistant principal finally reached Jamal's mom and shared Donald's idea, Jamal's mom said, "Mr. Donald can keep him there all night if it will stop you from calling me every day." She, like many parents, didn't quite know what to do with her pre-teen in one of the city's worst neighborhoods.

That day after school, Donald put Jamal to work—*serious work*. Trading in-school suspension for time with him wasn't meant to be a reward for Jamal. It was meant to redirect his actions. Donald placed particular emphasis on cleaning the classroom of the teacher who had sent Jamal to the assistant principal's office, and Jamal left a note on the chalkboard apologizing for the disruption. Donald was instinctively using restorative practices years before it was even considered a popular strategy. For him, it just made sense. If you commit a wrong, take responsibility and make it right.

At the end of the night, Jamal made a strange request. He asked Donald, "Can I come back and help you tomorrow?"

Donald replied, "Sure. I need all the help I can get. But you have to promise not to be sent out of class again. Deal?"

Jamal replied with an enthusiastic, "Deal!"

And so it began. Jamal stayed many nights at the school with Donald. He took cleaning breaks and did his homework. When homework and cleaning duties were complete, Donald would let Jamal go to the gym and play basketball at the end of Donald's shift.

The assistant principal was new to the job, but he was no fool. He soon realized that Donald had social capital in the neighborhood. That meant he was respected and trusted by its citizens. This kind of trust can go a long way and is worth your time to develop with members of your community. This is something you cannot buy in neighborhoods like that. One day the assistant principal asked Donald, "Do you need any more help at night? I've got about fourteen boys who don't seem to be responding to anything I do."

Donald answered, "Oh yeah! I'll put them all to work."

With the consent of parents, the boys were required to work with Donald after school. Sometimes there were up to seven kids cleaning the building, with Jamal acting as a peer-supervisor. Seeing that made Donald smile. But he had no idea of the impact he was having. Eventually, all fourteen boys mentioned by the assistant principal were required to work with Donald after school. And, like Jamal, many of them asked to come back.

One of the more interesting aspects of kids who show resilience is that they identify and recruit positive individuals into their lives.

Donald made the same deal with each of them. They could come back as long as they stayed out of trouble.

This went on for some time as the neighborhood continued to decline. One of the more interesting aspects of kids who show resilience is that they identify and recruit positive individuals into their lives.[12] And that is exactly what these boys were doing with Donald. The reason was simple. It wasn't about cleaning up the building. Although they loved the sport, it wasn't even about basketball. These boys wanted to stay after school with Donald because they were safer with him at the school than they were in some parts of their neighborhood. As he noticed crime increase, Donald became acutely aware that the school, particularly after hours, was a safe haven.

> ...changing the negative behaviors of just a few kids can sometimes change the culture of a building. It certainly can change the culture of a classroom.

Over the years, lots of kids followed Jamal's path and stayed after school to help Mr. Donald. What began as a punishment became an incentive that helped kids remain more socially and academically focused. Any assistant principal or dean of students can tell you that changing the negative behaviors of just a few kids can sometimes change the culture of a building. It certainly can change the culture of a classroom.

Let's be sure you see the connection between Donald's story and resilience. As previously stated in Chapter 2, resilience refers to the ability to avoid, bypass, navigate, bounce back from, get through, get over, go around, or survive adversities of all kinds. Applying this definition to Jamal and the other kids who worked with Donald, the behaviors that led to discipline referrals were a form of adversity. In other words, behavior was a risk factor for the students sent to Donald. The referrals were another form of adversity that may have resulted in lost instructional time. Donald's interaction with students helped them to avoid these risk factors. This was accomplished by incentivizing the students to exercise greater self-control and demonstrate more acceptable classroom behaviors. By doing this, the students displayed resilience. With the help of a caring adult, they avoided risk factors by exhibiting more positive behaviors. In addition to getting in the way of negative behaviors that often lead to less than desirable outcomes, Donald also got in the way of the many dangers most prevalent in areas where illegal drugs were bought and sold in communities. Donald's action served as a protective factor by mitigating the risks of negative behaviors and negative risk factors in the community.

To facilitate a deeper understanding of how resilience works, I offer this simple model. It is designed to show the interplay between risk factors and protective factors in the lives of children. Protective factors help children to bypass or bounce back from risk factors. Children who bypass or bounce back from risk factors are defined as resilient in the literature.[13] Consider the kids who stayed with Donald. On the left, you see the risk factors faced by the students. On the right, you see the protective factors. Donald and his willingness to use his influence in a creative way served as a significant buffer for the many kids who knew him. He got in the way of risk factors that could have literally killed these kids.

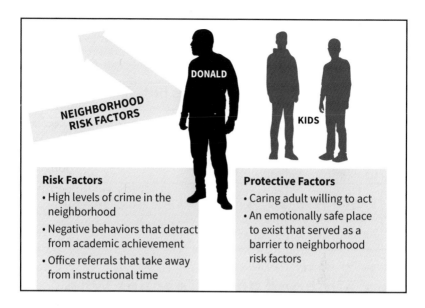

Risk Factors
- High levels of crime in the neighborhood
- Negative behaviors that detract from academic achievement
- Office referrals that take away from instructional time

Protective Factors
- Caring adult willing to act
- An emotionally safe place to exist that served as a barrier to neighborhood risk factors

As we consider ways in which schools and staff members can serve as protective factors for kids, it is important to note that there need not be a one-to-one ratio between risk factors and protective factors. Given what we know about the challenges faced daily in schools, this would not be practical. One of the most important elements in protecting kids from risk factors is the fidelity of the protective factor. How consistent is it? Can it be reliably deployed for maximum results? Protective factors must be consistent or else they will be less likely to have the desired impact on the life of a child. Going back to Donald's story, he was there at the school virtually every day. His actions were not written down in a manual, but they were systemic. *Systemic approaches are more likely to be effective in protecting children than sporadic events*. Events rarely change behavior; systemic strategies more often do. An end-of-year event

> *Protective factors must be consistent or else they will be less likely to have the desired impact on the life of a child.*

recognizing student achievement would not have been significant motivation for Donald's children. They needed an immediate, consistent intervention. Donald was it!

Roadblock Rules (R^2)

1.	Utilize effective instructional practices.
2.	Establish positive relationships with students that demonstrate genuine care and concern.
3.	Focus on systems, rather than events, to protect children.
4.	Be consistent with your actions.

My Childhood and a Teacher Who Got in the Way for Me

Do you ever get a chance to reflect on your childhood? I sure do. And there are aspects of my upbringing that I would not change for all the gold and silver in the world. Life up to second grade was like heaven to me. I am an African American child of the '60s and '70s, a unique time in our world's history. Looking back with adult eyes, I can see the challenges that existed in my hometown. But when I was a little boy, I had no idea these challenges existed. That's primarily because I was literally surrounded by love.

There was love for me in every house in my neighborhood. And like almost all of the kids where I lived, I had a nickname. Instead of being called John W. Hodge, I was John-John. I still get a warm feeling when I travel back home and the elders who are flourishing in their nineties call me John-John just like they did when I was a boy. My childhood was full of wonderful days in a neighborhood the likes of which rarely exist today.

My friends and I played outside every single day. Forgive me, my wonderful twentysomethings who may be digitally reading or listening to this book, but there was a time in America's history when we did not have computers in our homes. Telephones remained on wires. And unless you had a really long cord, they remained in one room. Our social media was something called a walkie-talkie. And those rarely worked if you were more than a hundred yards away from the friend with whom you were talking. It was just a different time. In many ways, it was a better time.

Imagine this with me. You are two blocks away from your house, and it's ninety degrees outside. We had no fear of the heat index. As a matter of fact, our mothers made us go outside to play in the summertime. After playing football outdoors for hours, you're too tired to walk all the way back home for a drink of something cool and refreshing. And instead of having to make that long walk back home, you can pick any one of ten homes filled with families who will gladly welcome you in for a nice, cool break before going back outdoors to finish the never-ending football game.

This will be hard for many of you to believe in today's harsh times, but I could walk into many of my neighbors' homes without even knocking. Mrs. Daisey Spruill was always cooking something fried and tasty. Today on my plant-based, hyper-healthy diet, I would probably have to pass on Mrs. Spruill's wonderful cooking. But I don't care who you are or how wealthy you might be, you haven't lived until you've had a pork chop from Miss Daisey.

Mrs. Mayes, another neighbor, had the best lemon iced tea. Again, reflecting on my childhood with my adult eyes and mature palate, I think Mrs. Mayes may have had a secret brew of sorts because her jars of what she called "secret tea" were really popular with the grown people. She once accidently gave me a sip of secret tea. Mrs. Mayes laughed until she cried, gave me a fresh glass of ice water and a kiss on the cheek, and sent me right back outside to finish the football game that never ended.

And here's a shocker for my younger readers: in our most desperate moments of being literally parched with thirst after hours of playing every outdoor game we could imagine, the boys and girls in our neighborhood would drink water straight from water hoses *without filters*. Things are so different now. Just a few years ago, when my nephew was a little boy, I once showed him how we drank from water hoses, and he cried thinking that his favorite uncle's demise was imminent. His combination of fear, love, and concern that day was absolutely adorable. And on that day, after we wiped his tears, he got a kiss on the cheek—just like the ones I used to get when I was a little boy like him.

Now that I've got you nice and thirsty, let me clarify the greatest drink in the history of my neighborhood. Thousands of you have probably heard this during one of my keynotes, but there was absolutely no comparison—not even secret tea—to the greatest drink ever made in the history of earth: Tang. Every kid in my old neighborhood preferred Tang for one simple reason. Have you ever seen the old Tang commercial? Well, my innocent six-year-old mind believed that if you drank just enough Tang, you could go fly on spaceships just like the astronauts in the commercial. So, in my old neighborhood, we were football-playing future astronauts on a daily diet of Tang. Heck, if Greg, Marcia, Peter, Jan, Bobby, and Cindy Brady of the then-famous Brady Bunch drank Tang, it was certainly good enough for us.

Another wonderful memory I have about my neighborhood is that all of the adults seemed to have good jobs. If they didn't work for a company, they worked for themselves as entrepreneurs. You didn't need to leave my street to get anything repaired. It didn't matter what it was, there was a repairman or woman for everything from your car to your roof to the toaster in your kitchen. You could get the best paint job for your house and have your front yard looking like Augusta National by doing business with your neighbors. Try finding that today. My grandfather warned that Americans were slowly becoming skill-less. I fear that there may have been some truth to his prognostication.

Our hometown had industries that would employ you for life, including steel, textiles, and the top of the economic food chain, tobacco. In 1969, you could graduate from high school with the level of skill expected from a graduate at that time and have a job with benefits within a week. If you were lucky enough to work for R. J. Reynolds Tobacco Company, your benefits package often included orthodontics for your entire family. You could always tell when a kid had parents who worked for RJR because of those steel traps called braces that eventually became beautiful smiles.

In December 1970, our utopian world began to change. On January 1, 1971, America saw its last televised cigarette commercial.[14] It was a subtle indicator of what was to follow. That last commercial signaled a change in the tobacco industry that would involve the public realization of the dangers of smoking. I guess the downward spiral of the industry may have begun in 1964 when the surgeon general publicly acknowledged the health risks of tobacco. Perhaps 1965 should have been a warning to those employed in the industry when Congress required all cigarette labels to include warnings to the public about the dangers of smoking. But who reads the small print when your livelihood, the very economic survival of your family, is dependent on an industry that has been deemed a health hazard?

I was old enough to remember the reaction to that final commercial. It was as if citizens knew the end was near. They even talked about it in church in a way that I did not quite understand until years later.

The tobacco industry did what most businesses do in challenging economic times. They protected their assets by downsizing. For neighborhoods like mine, that meant the jobs of our working adults were not protected. This time in my life gave me my first exposure to the phrase "last hired, first fired." This time-honored modus operandi used by many businesses in the South meant that some of the hardest-working people I've ever known lost their jobs and were unable to find economically comparable work. And just as we have witnessed later in history where local businesses quickly shut down, the impact on communities is fast and devastating. My city and the neighborhoods on my side of town never felt the same. The love and safety I once felt quickly turned into fear. I had great parents, but the circumstances I began to notice required someone outside my home to get in the way for me. Luckily for me, I found her. Or perhaps, she found me.

As neighborhoods began to decline, the streets we commonly played on became strange places. Many of the people we knew soon left and were replaced by people we did not know. There were times when we would see unfamiliar people come to our side of town and stand on corners. Soon after they took their positions on various corners, cars would begin to drive up and give the young men money. In return for the money, the people in the cars were given little bags. We were so innocent at that time; we did not realize that inside many of those little bags was the death of families in areas like mine: heroine.

Keeping us safe from harm was a challenging proposition for parents who maintained their jobs. Many of them, like my dad, did not get home from work until after nine o'clock. So parents did the best they could and told all of the kids who walked to school that we were never to walk alone in our neighborhood. This applied to elementary, middle, and high school students.

My group of buddies was pretty large, but for the purposes of this book, I'll condense and change the names. If you work with children, think about the kids you see every day. We were no different from them.

Eric	Business	Chris	Dead
John (Me)	Education	Terrance	Life in Prison
Drew	Business	Alan	Paroled Drug Addict
Paul	Medicine	Shawn	Life in Prison

This table represents some of my best friends in the world. We grew up together. We went to the same schools and lived in the same city. The data in the table displays two key factors about each of us. You see our first names and where we ended up in life. There are compelling stories and interesting facts about each of the names listed above. From a research standpoint, I fully realize that this is a very limited sample size. Though small, the group has unique characteristics, not the least of which is the fact that we attended the exact same elementary, junior high, and high schools. On a more humorous side, seven of the eight of us were born in August of the same year within a two-week period. Our best collective explanation is that the power went out one previous November weekend, and our parents had nothing else to do.

I feel strong emotions when I share my personal story because I believe with all of my heart that every little boy you see listed in the table should have become a successful adult. There are other powerful insights that can be gleaned from the careful analysis of the circumstances behind each result. But a philosophical rule referred to as Occam's razor offers me the clearest explanation for the disparate results on display. There are several interpretations of this philosophy, but the one that I think applies best here is the following: given a multitude of possible explanations, the simplest often best explains the most complex phenomenon.

In the case of my friends, Chris, the best athlete, was killed before his thirty-fifth birthday. Eric, a dreamer with very little noteworthy marketing abilities, became the owner of a successful car dealership. Paul grew up in the most horrendous circumstances of the entire group. His parents died when he was an infant, and he was raised by his elderly grandmother, who was constantly overwhelmed with medical and financial challenges. Paul was in my elementary class, and I distinctly remember that Paul could not read. Please don't misinterpret my last comment. Paul was not a struggling reader. Paul was illiterate when we were in grade school. Yet, years later, he graduated from one of the best premed programs in the world. He later attended medical school. And Paul, a former nonreader, has a thriving medical practice.

How in the world does this happen? What are the factors that contribute to the success or failure of our most vulnerable kids?

I searched many years for answers. It became somewhat of an obsession. After witnessing Chris's funeral and the way one bullet had ended his life, I always wondered why the stories of kids from virtually the exact same circumstances could follow drastically different pathways in life. My answer came in the most unlikely place.

The Date that Led to My Answer
My Mom, the Matchmaker

I eventually moved to Virginia, where my career in education soared. I was successful but I was not happy. I had endured some very challenging circumstances at that point in life. So, my mother, in her infinite wisdom, decided that it was time for me to get married. And Mom didn't just make the decision; she introduced me to a young lady and fellow educator named Richelle. We dated for a while and soon decided to tie the knot. It was a joyous occasion. We were joined by the people who meant the most to us throughout our lives. During the months leading up to my wedding, my mind occasionally drifted to my old friend Chris who was so brutally murdered. But I was determined not to allow that memory to ruin such a special time in my life. So, I buried it in my heart and did my best to enjoy all of the festivities. I am not a bachelor party guy, so in the weeks leading up to my wedding, a relative had a cookout for me. It was at this cookout that I discovered the answer to my life's most burning question: What was the key factor that differentiated the lives of my friends? The answer is consistent with the overwhelming conclusion found in much of the resilience research. The entire trajectory of a child's life can be changed for the better due to the actions of one caring adult.[15]

On the night of the cookout, a close relative gave us a generous supply of what I called "secret tea" earlier in this book. I think to honor the best drink we ever had in our neighborhood growing up, I will simply call it a very special and robust version of Tang that is made in the hills of North Carolina by people who specialize in making strong beverages. So, there we were, drinking "Tang" and talking about life. Eventually we arrived at the topic I had buried deeply in my heart, Chris. We spent time consuming more and more Tang and becoming more philosophical with each sip. I even mentioned Occam's razor a few times in ways that didn't fit. Then, all of the sudden, it happened: the answer I was chasing, the secret that explained how some individuals transcend difficult circumstances while so many others fall tragically short. My answer came in the form of a question asked by Paul.

Fully overflowing with Tang to the point at which his perspiration almost appeared to have an orange hue, Paul asked me a serious question. His query began with a request. Paul said, "John-John, don't take this the wrong way." It's been my experience that when a question is preceded with an introduction such as this, it's probably a good idea to brace your emotions. But Tang or no Tang, Paul was on to something that night.

After his brief introduction, he began his question. "John-John, people actually pay you to speak?" The inflection in his voice was indicative of his amazement that such a thing could be true. And I must admit that the Tang in me made me feel a bit defensive. I began to give Paul my verbal resume of the things I had accomplished. But Paul would not allow me to finish my response. He replied, "No! You're taking it the wrong way! I just want to be clear that you are compensated to talk to large audiences."

To his comment, I replied with a simple yes, followed by, "I am often compensated to speak to groups of all types."

Then a strange emotional response that I wasn't expecting came from Paul and was joined by others present. Paul said, "John-John, didn't you stutter or have some kind of speech impediment when we were very little? I mean, seriously man, I don't recall how your voice sounded." He continued, "As a matter of fact, I can't remember how you sounded because I rarely heard you say a word." Paul was right. But something much bigger had just happened in that moment of clarity. And if you have ever doubted your ability to make a difference in the life of a child, this is the moment that doubt ends.

Allow me to explain what was happening in the conversation between Paul and me. And I want you to remember it for the rest of your life.

On the night Paul asked me these questions, here is what was actually happening:

A little boy who could not read was asking a little boy who could not speak, *How in the world did we get here? What was it?* And within the context of this book, Paul was asking, *Who got in the way for us?* The answer will motivate many of you and perhaps frustrate others. It all depends on how you view the chart. And, as Occam's razor suggests, the answer is rather simple yet extremely powerful. Here it is:

Mrs. Dawson		Other Teachers	
Eric	Business	Chris	Dead
John (Me)	Education	Terrance	Life in Prison
Drew	Business	Alan	Paroled Drug Addict
Paul	Medicine	Shawn	Life in Prison

In elementary school, all of the boys on the left side of the chart had the same teacher, Mrs. Geraldine Dawson. For the record, Mrs. Dawson did not care what the teacher who had you last year said about you. She cared even less about how your house or neighborhood looked. At that time, Mrs. Dawson was the only teacher we had who cared enough to visit our neighborhood. Mrs. Dawson serves as motivation for me every day of my life. She was the one who made me give my first speech in public. She treated all students with overt kindness on a daily basis. When she disciplined us, she made it clear that she disliked our behavior but still loved us. She made lessons interesting, which made learning easier. And regardless of our academic ability, Mrs. Dawson made us feel smart.

Paul can still recall the very day Mrs. Dawson began to change his life. It was the first day of school. As was customary on the first day, teachers clarified your full name, address, and home phone number for contact information. As she went down the list of names that day, Paul became more nervous as with each name she came closer to his. When she finally arrived at Paul's name, she repeated the same questions she had asked everyone. She asked for his full name, address, and phone number. Paul did fine with the first two questions. But the third question was almost too much for him to answer. He tried quietly at first. Mrs. Dawson replied, "Speak up, sweetie, so I can hear you."

That is when Paul was forced to utter words that may have changed his life. They certainly impacted his relationship with Mrs. Dawson. Paul had to announce to the entire class, "I'm sorry Mrs. Dawson, but I don't have a phone." I remember hearing someone snicker at Paul's embarrassment. It certainly was not someone from our neighborhood. But it still hurt deeply. Yet to this day, I don't know who was hurt more, Paul or Mrs. Dawson. All I know is that later that day after school as we played ball outside, a red car with an elephant on the dashboard drove down our street.

We were in shock. It was her. Mrs. Dawson came to our street. She drove past us, waved, smiled, and headed to Paul's grandmother's house. We will never know the complete details of the conversation between these two women, but one comment we do know came from Mrs. Dawson. According to Paul and his brother, Mrs. Dawson apologized for the question and then told Paul's grandmother that she believed Paul was college material. She believed that fact despite the appearance of his home and the obvious lack of resources. She knew in her heart that Paul, who could not read in the second grade, could one day be a college graduate. And for the rest of that year, and several years that followed, Mrs. Dawson got in the way of the risk factors that should have held Paul back.

> *Her actions prove that if a child is fortunate enough to meet the right adult at the right time who is willing to get in the way of risk factors, the entire trajectory of that child's life can change.*

Her actions prove that if a child is fortunate enough to meet the right adult at the right time who is willing to get in the way of risk factors, the entire trajectory of that child's life can change. And I will go to my grave believing that if Chris had been in her class, he would still be alive today. Because there is no doubt in my mind that Mrs. Dawson would have gotten in the way of his risk factors just as she did for the rest of us. She is a wonderful example of what a teacher who's following the first four rules might do.

Implementation Imperatives: Rules #3 and #4

For the purposes of our discussion, systems are ongoing practices and procedures that take place consistently. Instead of one-week sprints, systems are year-long marathons. We'll collapse rules 3 and 4 and discuss them simultaneously. It's logical that a school attempting to improve attendance might schedule a onetime event to recognize students who achieve attendance goals. However, onetime events won't yield the same results as daily reminders, acknowledgments, and discussions on a consistent basis. This consistency means every day of the week for many schools. Consider the following scenario.

A school board votes on a new policy that will require students to attend one day of Saturday school for every four unexcused absences from school. To avoid the need for students to attend

Saturday school, one middle school did the following:

- They announced the new policy to students and parents
- They placed the policy on the school's website
- They planned an incentivized celebration for the end of the grading period for students who achieved the goal

These are great ideas. However, in the scenario described above, the school has essentially implemented three events. These are not systemic strategies. In order to make success more likely, the school should first analyze trend data to determine if existing strategies are working. Research strategies that have yielded desired results in schools that serve a similar demographic. Implement strategies on an ongoing basis. Again, if we want students to achieve a daily goal, it makes no sense to remind and incentivize them on a quarterly basis. Schools are far more likely to achieve results when efforts are systemic and used consistently.

To help ensure that best practices are shared with colleagues for school-wide impact, we've added a fifth rule.

Roadblock Rules (R^2)

1.	Utilize effective instructional practices.
2.	Establish positive relationships with students that demonstrate genuine care and concern.
3.	Focus on systems, rather than events, to protect children.
4.	Be consistent with your actions.
5	Be willing to collaborate with others to ensure school-wide norms.

Implementation Imperatives: Rule #5

To ensure that you, the reader, have a clear understanding, we will discuss rule number five in the current chapter and very briefly expand on this at the end of Chapter 4. This is done to show that these rules are interdependent in many ways. Strict compartmentalization of ideas is ultimately counterproductive.

We've all heard of the importance of creating communities of learners. Unfortunately, learning communities are often defined so broadly that they lose their meaning in many ways. Still, their purpose remains powerful. Whether you connect with colleagues via grade-level teams, subject-area groups, or departments, working together is essential. If something is working, please share it with others.

- Introduce the idea, concept, or strategy
- Review the protocols for implementation
- Discuss its pros and cons
- Try it
- Discuss the results
- Try it again

The work of Joyce and Showers (2002) suggests that ongoing dialogue with colleagues is the key to successful implementation of new ideas and strategies.[16]

If the size of your school or dynamics of your school's culture force you to fly solo, don't stress out. Social media platforms offer wonderful opportunities to collaborate with others who share your passion. And it's often the case that the success of individuals serves as a motivating factor for others within a school to attempt new things. You are never alone. There are others just like you who want to get in the way.

SAME
(Social, Academic,
Moral Education):
A Systemic Way You Can
Get in the Way

The daily challenges we face in schools can seem overwhelming. We must collectively have the ability and willingness to *empathize* with the students we serve. However, it is of paramount importance that we not allow our empathy to progress into the type of crippling pity that often hinders our ability to take action. Put simply, you can't get in the way if you are blinded by circumstances.

> *Put simply, you can't get in the way if you are blinded by circumstances.*

The adults in schools must be able to see beyond current circumstances. If we can't, kids won't. In the comprehensive training program our company offers on how to thrive during turbulent times, I draw up the experiences of our organization during our extensive work with schools that endured the challenges of Hurricane Katrina. Helping adults and students see beyond the difficulties of current circumstances is of primary importance if we ever hope to help them reach their fullest potential. Current challenges in school culture and disappointing achievement levels are temporary stops on our collective journey toward excellence.

> *...when we allow current circumstances faced by our students to justify their negative behaviors and low academic achievement, **we are simply loving children into failure.***

I know you love your students. If you didn't, you wouldn't be reading this book. But when we allow current circumstances faced by our students to justify their negative behaviors and low academic achievement, *we are simply loving children into failure*. To love a child means to expect their best. Children who demonstrate resilience are surrounded by adults who have high expectations of them despite risk factors. When these adults act systemically with love and support, greater numbers of students are able to transcend the most challenging circumstances.

The systemic approach that guides the work of my company (Urban Learning and Leadership Center) is called SAME. We at ULLC have a well-documented record of helping to create school-wide cultures in which children and adults thrive despite a variety of challenges thanks largely to our SAME (Social, Academic, Moral Education) model. This research-supported model has impacted over 246,000 students in 494 US schools.

SAME is a systemic and holistic approach to educating children that strengthens resilience, enhances social-emotional development, and raises academic achievement by helping to create safe learning environments for children of all ages, particularly those at high risk of social and academic failure. In his book *On Purpose: How Great School Cultures Form Strong Character*, best-selling author Samuel Casey Carter showcased the SAME model as one of America's twelve most exciting approaches that should be replicated by educators for its success and sustainability.[17]

Embedded within the SAME framework is social-emotional learning (SEL), defined by the Wallace Foundation as "the process through which individuals learn and apply a set of social, emotional, and related skills, attitudes, behaviors, and values that help direct their thoughts, feelings, and actions in ways that enable them to succeed in school, work, and life."[18]

If the term *social-emotional learning* makes your community uncomfortable, use "life skills" as a description. The bottom line is that we want students to be equipped to make the right decisions and enter adulthood prepared for the challenges of life—full stop.

Within each of the domains of the SAME framework—social, academic, and moral—there are aspects that apply to the students in the building and aspects that apply to adults. For successful implementation, all three domains (social, academic, and moral) must be addressed within a culture of distributed leadership. This means that we are united by a common mission and vision. It also means that all of the kids in the school belong to all of us, regardless of the grade level or subject area. This is true whether you're in a K–12 school with three hundred students or a 9–12 school with three thousand. While success is typically a collaborative effort, you can follow SAME on your own. When you succeed, others will follow.

SAME was first piloted in Newport News Public Schools at An Achievable Dream Academy. At the time, the K–8 public school had nearly one thousand students. That population represented subgroups that traditionally underperform and are often tragically underserved. As a result, they often achieve at levels far below their potential. Over 95 percent of its students were

African American and impoverished. Approximately 89 percent of its students came from single-parent households. Many of them lived in less-than-ideal housing. Despite these risk factors, the school became one of the highest-performing schools in the Commonwealth of Virginia.

I played an important role in the initial development and implementation of the SAME framework. The company for which I have worked over twenty years, ULLC, was originally established to share SAME with schools throughout the United States. This important work has taken us to all types of schools in a variety of school districts. Our longitudinal data supports one powerful conclusion: if you truly want to achieve and sustain excellence for all students in a school, you must work holistically. SAME offers those who work with students a pathway to sustainable success.

The efficacy of the SAME model was demonstrated in a statewide reform effort with the Louisiana High Performing / High Poverty Schools (HPHP) Initiative, a collaborative effort between ULLC, the Wallace Foundation, and the Louisiana State Department of Education (LDOE). The effort provided targeted support to schools serving the state's most vulnerable students. This important work received high praise for the progress made in high-poverty schools throughout the state. According to Board of Elementary and Secondary Education president Penny Dastugue, "Their demonstrated success is evidence that schools can perform at high levels, even under the most challenging circumstances."[19] As a result of this intensive effort, the number of high-poverty schools designated as high performing nearly doubled across the entire state. Culture is only the first step. The ultimate target is student achievement followed by success in society.

In Tangipahoa Parish, a high-poverty district severely impacted by Katrina, data indicated that cultural changes occurred in High

Priority schools. These changes were statistically significant. Impoverished African American students in writing and math closed achievement gaps with their more affluent white counterparts. This was accomplished despite the risk factors that often prevent desired achievement levels.

The Social Domain: The S in SAME

Given our extensive experiences in urban, rural, and suburban schools, we realize that every school has its own unique culture that includes a social domain. We define the social domain as the manner in which members of the school community behave. We all realize that negative behaviors are a significant risk factor for millions of students. These behaviors may lead to negative outcomes. This highlights why it is imperative that we get in the way of negative behaviors to prevent this type of end result.

BE What You Want Students to BECOME

Normally, when you use the words *school* and *behavior* in the same sentence, people assume that you are referring to the students within the school. In this case, I am. However, the focus on behavior within schools must go beyond students. To be quite honest, I've been in lots of schools across the country with toxic cultures where the source of the problem was not the kids. In many cases, the behavior of the adults in the building was a much bigger challenge to overcome.

Many professionals involved in the field of education don't realize that children in K–12 schools model what they see. In other words, what they see is what they do. Therefore, if we want kids to show up to school on time with positive attitudes, *we the adults must show up to school on time with positive attitudes.* If we are serious about improving the culture of a school, and truly getting in the way of behavioral risk factors, we must overtly and consistently model the behaviors we desire. When this happens, the school's culture becomes a buffer to the negative behaviors kids often see in homes, communities, and on social media. The school's positive culture literally gets in the way of the negative examples of behavior that children often see in other environments. The same applies to your individual classrooms. Some schools aren't designed for large-scale collaborative efforts. If that's the case in your school, focus on applying these ideas to your individual classroom.

Make a list of the behaviors you desire from your students. On the left side of a page, write the behaviors you would like to see from students. On the right side of the page, write the ways they are currently modeled by the adults in the building. These first two steps alone are a modified gap analysis. Schools often have a robust left side of the page. Unfortunately, the right side of the page is all too often sparse at best. But don't worry. This is simply an opportunity for growth.

If you're able to work with a team, discuss these ideas. Debate them if you must. If you already have a list, fantastic. The next step is crucial whether you are working with elementary, middle, or high school students. After the list is complete, ask yourself the following questions:

- What can I/we do to consistently and specifically model these behaviors in our school on a daily basis?
- What are our potential entry points to discuss and/or demonstrate these behaviors?
- Are there current programs, procedures, or customs we can build on to address desired behaviors?
- How can we leverage student leaders to enhance our effort?

It is often the case that when I ask this question during meetings with schools, I get very little response at first. There is often a long pause. Despite the discomfort a staff may feel when addressing the questions, the reason this discussion is so important is rather simple. Regardless of which behaviors we want from our students, we must be mindful that *students must see them from us before they can show them to us.*

In my experience, *respect* is the most common term listed as a desired behavior or character trait by school faculties. But trust me, students won't show it to you until they receive it from you. As a school leader, I wanted my students to show respect to the adults in our building. For this very reason, I treated students and other adults in the building with overt respect. I responded to questions from our custodians with "Yes, sir" and "No, sir." For kids, seeing respect in action on a daily basis can impact their behavior in positive ways by getting in the way of negative behavioral examples often seen by students elsewhere.

There are literally thousands of programs designed to impact student behavior. Regardless of which program or approach has been adopted by your school or district, I've found that restorative practices that emphasize the emotional well-being of students provide the best long-term benefits. The best approaches do the following:

1. Tell students what the behavioral expectations are
2. Explain why the desired behaviors are relevant
3. Show and/or model desired behaviors
4. Affirm students when they display or demonstrate desired behaviors
5. Correct students when they fall short of behavioral expectations

6. Encourage students to take responsibility

7. Involve communities in the process when possible

8. Repeat these steps over and over and over

I assure you that my ultimate goal is to help you thrive, not sell you a program. SAME is not a program for sale. It's an approach that anyone can use to guide your actions in a school. Access to information is rarely the main challenge for schools. In districts throughout the country, products that are often purchased at significant expense are not the main hurdle. One of the most common challenges I've seen in hundreds of schools is *fidelity of implementation*. This reality is often complicated by a lack of training. Teachers are given a one-hour training at the end of the day on a Friday and are expected to fully implement Monday morning. If you are a leader, don't waste your time and money. Know this: regardless of the program you are attempting to implement, I assure you with near certainty that if there is no follow-up or ongoing discussion of program elements, there will be no fidelity. If you, your school, or district commits to a program, give it time to work. There are no magic bullets. Even the best approaches take time.

After the commitment to time has been established, ask for entry points for training and support. Trust me, you'll need it. Grade-level meetings, professional learning community (PLC) meetings, department meetings, professional development sessions, and job-embedded support from specialists are just a few ways you can ensure the approaches you select have a chance to make the impact you desire. If resources and information are unavailable on-site, use web-based supports. The last thing we want is for a great idea to fail because we lack the support and/or the patience required for success. Too often, when ideas fail, so do our kids.

The Academic Domain:
The A in SAME

As stated previously, SAME is a holistic approach. Addressing behavioral expectations within the social domain is crucial. But you can't stop there. After all, we work in schools, not social clubs. We cannot prepare students for life after school without addressing the academic domain within the school. The academic domain in SAME refers to the manner in which members of the school community engage in teaching and learning.

In a book I coauthored called *Standing in the Gap: A Guide to Using the SAME Framework to Create Excellent Schools*, we spend significant time addressing the pedagogical essentials for high-quality instruction. Many of the teachers we encounter in our work as consultants seem most comfortable with this aspect of their job. For this reason, I've decided to approach the academic domain of SAME in a way that addresses the emotional realities of what we see in schools that impact this domain.

The social and emotional impediments experienced by children and adults in today's schools can have long-lasting detrimental effects on our progress in the academic domain. It is a drastic error to separate emotions from the learning process. I know teachers who have lost spouses and children who have lost parents. The fact that these circumstances may have a detrimental impact on teaching and learning is irrefutable. A greater understanding of the impact of stress on the brain may pay academic dividends in the future. Teachers who have a better understanding of trauma and its impact on social and emotional development are much more likely to get in the way of risk factors that may impede the learning process. Children can't learn and teachers can't teach if they are extremely stressed or afraid.

Urban Learning and Leadership Center has a Family Services division that operates with the sole purpose of providing mental health support services to children and families. Although I was primarily trained as a teacher, the growth in my understanding of mental health, and my research of resilience, has made me a more effective educator. Equipped with this knowledge, teachers can make classrooms havens of support by simply acquiring more knowledge about how the human brain functions.

The old days of teachers who brag about the level of stress they levy on their students should be long gone based on what we now know about the brain. Stress has a detrimental impact on the ability to learn. And it is important to note that this often cannot be controlled by the student. When a human being becomes stressed, levels of cortisol build in the bloodstream. Fear, worry, and anger are just a few of the triggers that can cause this biological response in the body. As the cortisol increases, it begins to eat or destroy glucose. This may sound minor, and thankfully it's not a life-threatening phenomenon, but it does hinder the process of learning because glucose is a primary fuel for the brain. As the cortisol consumes glucose, the brain literally has less fuel. To give you context, imagine a car attempting to function without gasoline. That's similar to what happens to the brain when a person is stressed. For this reason, educators must do all that they can to de-escalate stress so that the brains of students can function at optimal levels.

Simple Ways to De-Escalate Stress for Students in the Classroom:

- Treat all students with kindness and respect at all times
- Be clear about expectations
- Encourage students to take academic risks

- Praise effort as much as end results
- Offer students multiple avenues to seek and receive support
- Provide students a variety of ways to succeed in your class

As we remain in our discussion of the academic domain within the SAME framework, keep in mind that the ability to cope with unexpected circumstances is regarded as an important resilience that can be taught to children and adults. Meditation, for example, is a de-escalation technique that can assist individuals to successfully navigate difficult emotional circumstances. If the term *meditation* is taboo in your community, *focused thought* and *calmness* work just fine. Don't let semantics prevent success.

This past year, I provided seminars to entire schools on how to create classroom climates for State and AP testing, which are both known to cause high levels of stress in students, especially those who aspire to attend college. To the extent possible, schools must also remain void of negative triggers. Within the context of our academic domain discussion, I am referring to mental triggers that increase levels of stress. Among the most common triggers are the following:

- unpredictability
- sensory overload
- fear

Similar to the impact on brain function when glucose is lost, the triggered brain is extremely difficult to teach. In many cases, the triggered individual has difficulty accessing regions of the brain that control reason and higher-level thinking. The triggered brain needs a roadblock that will mitigate risk factors that negatively impact learning. Starting with a stress-free, emotionally safe, and bully-proof classroom may have a significantly positive impact on brain function and learning.

Trigger	Ways You Can Get in the Way
Unpredictability	• Establish daily classroom rituals and clear expectations • Post student-friendly learning targets on a daily basis to mitigate uncertainty • Create and follow a classroom calendar
Sensory overload	• Collapse lessons and content into manageable learning chunks • Give students more than one way to acquire knowledge
Feelings of vulnerability, frustration, fear	• Commend students as often as you can • Encourage students when they experience disappointment • Make sure your class is a bully-free zone • Schedule multiple opportunities for student success • Keep stakeholders informed to the extent possible

These ideas will help the brain remain in a learning mode instead of a triggered mode. The default disposition of the triggered mind is often fight or flight, a mental state in which learning is unlikely. This explains why something as simple as a learning target can positively impact brain function by giving children an idea of what to expect during the lesson.

The Moral Domain: The M in SAME

We will conclude our discussion of the three domains by briefly touching on the moral domain of SAME. In the interest of full disclosure, I must admit that of the three domains—social, academic, and moral—the moral domain typically causes the most consternation from faculty, but it may be the most important domain because it involves what we believe.

The social and moral domains are impossible to separate, which is why some call this domain the social-emotional domain. Dr. Harvey Perkins, CEO of ULLC, offers an explanation that brings a degree of clarity to the two domains. According to Dr. Perkins, the social domain is all about the external, while the moral domain is all about the internal. The things we believe dramatically impact the things we do. In other words, what we believe internally drives what we do externally. For those who struggle with negative beliefs about children and their ability to achieve, Robert Marzano offers a wonderful suggestion in *The Art and Science of Teaching*.[20] Marzano recommends that adults acknowledge their low expectations and negative beliefs to themselves, then act in complete contradiction to the negative belief. If, for example, you have trouble believing that certain students can achieve academic standards, acknowledge that belief to yourself but treat the kids as if you believe they can surpass the standards. Act in contradiction to your negative beliefs.

Roadblock Rules (R^2)

1.	Utilize effective instructional practices.
2.	Establish positive relationships with students that demonstrate genuine care and concern.
3.	Focus on systems, rather than events, to protect children.
4.	Be consistent with your actions.
5	Be willing to collaborate with others to ensure school-wide norms.
6.	Give your new approaches time to work.

Implementation Imperatives: Rules #5 and #6

I've seen collaboration defined in a variety of ways. One of the most creative and clear definitions came from my former mentor, Dr. Thelma Spencer-Hamrick. Thelma, cofounder of our company and former counselor, defined collaboration as one's willingness to give help when asked and to ask for help when in need. Isolation is a zero-sum game in the field of education. As mentioned earlier in the chapter, this is true for the rules as much as it is true for those attempting to implement the rules. Our jobs are simply too difficult for us to succeed by working in isolation. Look for opportunities to share and receive ideas. This is essential.

Members of our teams should feel comfortable enough to ask for help or to admit confusion. This may require that a group work on trust first. But after trust is established, the sky is the limit. Mrs. Dawson taught me almost half a century ago that you grow when you admit you don't know. It was true in elementary school, and it's certainly true in my corporate office.

Patience is a virtue in many fields of practice. It's common nature to lose patience in the beginning of an initiative and never give ourselves time to work out the kinks. Change that really matters takes time. Don't be afraid to give your efforts time to work.

6 Key Steps to Successful Planning

By now you may be thinking, *Okay, John, we want to get in the way. How do we start?* Our approach at ULLC is among the most distinctive of its kind. We simply do not believe in cookie-cutter, one-size-fits-all approaches to improving schools. There is simply too much variability within schools and districts to rely on strategies that treat them as if they are all the same. Instead, we carefully tailor interventions to fit the specific needs of the school. You can do the same in your classroom.

> *There is simply too much variability within schools and districts to rely on strategies that treat them as if they are all the same.*

Our process begins with a comprehensive diagnostic evaluation and ends with a report that includes specific recommendations to move the school toward desired results. Three areas of discovery guide the development of the report. These discovery areas can be used by any school or individual to guide your own self-assessment. Using data to guide your discoveries, consider the following areas to begin the process of improvement.

Discovery Areas for School Diagnosis

DISCOVERY AREA **1**	What are my building blocks of success? These are the things I am currently doing well that can be leveraged for greater improvement.
DISCOVERY AREA **2**	Where are my opportunities for growth? These are the things that could improve school climate and student achievement if properly addressed.
DISCOVERY AREA **3**	Based on data, immediate needs, and resources, what are my immediate next steps? These are the first three to five essential steps that must be taken to address your most pressing needs.

Nothing Happens Without an Action Plan: 6 Key Steps to Success

Urban Learning and Leadership Center works collaboratively with schools and district staff to develop clear, concise action documents that clarify focus. Teachers cannot be expected to implement a plan they've never seen or helped to develop. The planning process is so important because it prevents what we noticed in Mrs. Dawson's story. In that school, there were obviously good strategies in use. The tragedy was that not every child had access to those strategies. An even more tragic possibility is the fact that the teachers themselves may have been unable or unaware of the most effective ways to impact student achievement. To ensure that our expectations and strategies become common knowledge, we use a simple six-step process to enhance the likelihood of implementation.

This six-step process helps schools and individual educators implement programs, processes, and procedures designed to focus efforts so that valuable time will not be lost.

1. Data Capture and Reporting
2. Data Analysis
3. Goal/Objective Setting, Evidence of Success
4. Strategy/Action Plan Development
5. Monitoring and Adjusting
6. Communicating the Plan

Keep in mind this is a process, not a program. The real value of the process is the analysis, reflection, and dialogue that must take place to complete it. Heavy emphasis should be placed on steps 1, 3, and 5. Schools can become so overwhelmed with data that they suffer from analysis paralysis. Clearly decide which data sets will drive your plan of action and stick with it. In steps 3 and 4, make sure that your action steps are directly aligned with the data you are attempting to improve. When steps 3 and 4 are misaligned, success is highly unlikely. Step 5 is where most schools fall short. We sometimes become so engrossed with surviving week to week that we forget to monitor the implementation of the plan. Are we doing what we said we would do? What gets monitored gets done. Let me be clear—all six steps are essential. I highlight steps 1, 3, and 5 because these are areas that seem to be most challenging for a significant number of schools. Step 6 should be simple. Communicate key aspects of your plan with key stakeholders. Use a variety of methods: email, social media, phone calls, snail mail, and so on. Do whatever it takes to include stakeholders in the effort. Get everyone on the same page and make a difference for students.

Six-Step Action Planning Template

Goal Target: Chronic Absenteeism

Statement/Evidence of Need (Data Capture/Analysis - Steps 1 & 2)	(Step 3) Objective A
A.	
The Format can Be Changed	(Step 3) Objective A
B.	Objective B

Action Steps/ Strategies (Step 4)	Monitoring (Step 5)						
	Need? A or B	Person(s) Responsible	Team Members	Resources/ Staff Development Needed	Evidence	Reporting Timeframe	Completion Date
1.							
2.							
3.							
4.							
5.							
6.							
7.							

(Step 6): How will we communicate the plan? (Use back of page if needed)

_____

_____

_____

Implementation Imperatives: Rule #7

Keep in mind that the six-step process is not exclusively for addressing academic issues. We've seen it successfully deployed to address a variety of challenges. Strategies that seem small and insignificant can have the biggest impact on preventing risk factors from destroying the lives of kids.

I've been associated with several schools that decided, based on careful data analysis, that they needed a more structured way to start school. An Achievable Dream Academy had similar challenges. This issue is certainly not unique. Several schools in

Louisiana and Virginia noticed that disruptive behavior was more likely to occur at the beginning of the day when students entered the building from the bus or the community. Sometimes fights from the neighborhood would spill over into the school. This is common in many neighborhoods.

Using the six-step process, schools captured the data relative to student behavior at the very beginning of the day. This included horseplaying in the hallway, being tardy for the first class, disruptive behavior in the cafeteria, arguments on the bus, and so on. This is step 1.

Steps 2 and 3 involve data analysis and setting a measurable objective (SMART) goal. SMART is an acronym for **S**pecific, **M**easurable, **A**chievable, **R**ealistic, and **T**imely. If you don't have a problem, a SMART goal is unnecessary. It's quite possible that a negative assumption is proven false through the careful analysis of data. Don't you love it when that happens? If a challenge is discovered, set the goal you would like to reach. This might involve attendance improvement, a reduction in tardiness, reductions in truancy, fewer student conflicts, or a variety of other issues that may be important links to your school's mission and vision.

Step 4 is where the dialogue gets fun and interesting. This step is where individuals, teams, and/or school leaders begin to list effective strategies that the entire staff will endorse and take an active role in completing. Keep in mind when you decide on strategies, *less is more*. It is far better to list two to three high-yield strategies that can be implemented and monitored effectively than to list twenty strategies that were most likely compiled by the two people who were tasked with completing the plan and submitting it to the district office. Plans like that don't get implemented and they don't get in the way of the risk factors that negatively impact the children we so desperately want to support.

Morning strategies that I've seen effectively set the tone for the school include

- Morning welcomes (either in person or via TV monitors)
- Morning meetings in homeroom
- Morning classes for character development and social-emotional support
- Morning news broadcast
- Character and culture reminders to focus kids on acceptable behaviors and desired goals

Steps 5 and 6 involve monitoring and communicating the plan. If, for example, a strategy is not working, wouldn't you rather find out in the first three weeks of school rather than January? Communicating has a dual purpose. There may be key stakeholders who need to know how they can help to support your efforts. Relax! You certainly do not need to disclose every element of the plan. You decide what elements of the plan are essential for success and move forward with sharing those elements of your action plan.

Let's go back to step 4 for a moment. During this step, individuals or teams decide which strategies they will use to address the challenges discovered as a result of data analysis. The morning handshake has been a very popular strategy in many of the schools I've supported. It wouldn't be shocking to me if a person trivialized a strategy like a simple handshake. I completely understand that it is easy to become so frustrated and jaded that you doubt if anything will work. I've been in that place at a point in my career. But let me explain the efficacy and impact of that simple strategy by sharing Robert's story.

One Simple Strategy Helped to Get in the Way of Robert's Risk Factors

One Monday, one of Robert's teachers noticed during the morning welcome that he looked different. He seemed stressed or worried. Being worried in elementary school is not abnormal. There are lots of things that can impact the way a child feels on a given day. When asked what was bothering him, Robert quietly responded that he was unable to wake his mother. A matter of minutes after he spoke those words, the school received a phone call in the office from one of Robert's neighbors. Although the neighbor was pleased that Robert had made it to school, she shared the tragic news. The reason Robert was unable to wake his mother was because she had overdosed on heroine.

On Friday night, Robert watched his mother take her medicine (heroine) and fall into what appeared to young Robert to be a deep sleep. On Saturday morning, Robert attempted to wake his mother. After being unable to wake her, Robert ate cereal and watched TV. Saturday night was quiet, and Robert began to worry a bit. But he had seen his mother sleep for long periods of time and wake up. So, he naturally assumed that she would eventually rise from her slumber. Eight-year-old Robert was again unable to wake his mother on Sunday. On Monday, he tried a final time to wake her, and being unaware of what decomposition meant, he told his mother to take a bath. He then dressed himself and walked to school.

When asked why he came to school, Robert replied, "Because I knew my teacher would be waiting for me." Having a strong connection to a teacher meant everything to a little boy who had no place else to go. And the adults in his school got in the way of further risk factors he may have suffered if he had endured this horrible tragedy without their support. On the days that followed, he continued showing up to school. The simple idea that a caring person would be waiting for him helped to remove him from a horrible situation and begin the long process of emotional healing that followed. Robert's story epitomizes the resilience phenomenon. A little boy who lost his mother to a tragic overdose made it to school, continued to attend, and eventually graduated because caring adults got in the way of his risk factors.

Having a trauma-informed background is extremely helpful when attempting to address the challenges we face in high-poverty schools. Without such knowledge, our first inclination is to try to punish away the problem. Dr. Thelma Spencer-Hamrick, cofounder of Urban Learning and Leadership Center, was emphatic with her admonishment to new administrators about her fundamental belief that "a school cannot suspend and expel its way to excellence." Few statements on school culture ring truer than that bit of wisdom. Data-driven programs, processes, and strategies are the most effective ways to impact school culture, especially when children enter the building with levels of stress that are beyond burdens felt by most adults.

Conclusion

Before we conclude, let's look at the rules one last time.

Roadblock Rules (R^2)

1.	Utilize effective instructional practices.
2.	Establish positive relationships with students that demonstrate genuine care and concern.
3.	Focus on systems, rather than events, to protect children.
4.	Be consistent with your actions.
5	Be willing to collaborate with others to ensure school-wide norms.
6.	Give your new approaches time to work.
7.	Use available data and follow the six essential steps for planning.

We've covered significant ground. I am honored that you have decided to remain on this journey with me thus far. This in an introductory book on the resilience phenomenon with simple strategies to help support it in our students. More books will follow. We've discussed a few essentials for effective classroom instruction. Let's remember that those essentials were offered with the assumption of a teacher having access to curricula that is aligned with state standards. The stories of Donald Humphrey and James Hayden offer practical ways to facilitate better relationships with kids. Consistently showing kindness and offering a structured, safe place with a caring adult can help get in the way of a variety of risk factors. You don't necessarily need a set of complex skills to begin. All you need is the will to act. As we seek to improve the lives of children, we must remember that we are all learners. The more we share and collaborate, the better off we are. I believe this to be true in every industry. Our collective success also requires patience as silver bullet solutions simply do not exist for our most difficult issues in education. Finally, the use of data and planning in our efforts to identify and address student needs is imperative. These simple ideas used by an individual, a grade level, or department can enhance resilience in students and make success in life more likely. I have no doubt you can do it. You have more than enough talent. Don't worry about being an expert. Just start and you'll be shocked at what you discover. You and you alone may be their best hope. And please know that I'll be praying for you and, if needed, helping you along the way. You were made for this moment!

I look forward to hearing about the ways you're able to mitigate risk factors. Together, we can make success more likely for millions of children. So go GET IN THE WAY of risk factors for your students.

Notes

1. Werner and Smith, *Overcoming the Odds*.
2. Wolin and Wolin, *The Resilient Self*.
3. Werner and Smith, *Overcoming the Odds*; and Wolin and Wolin, *The Resilient Self*.
4. Wolin and Wolin, *The Resilient Self*.
5. National Scientific Council on the Developing Child, "Young Children Develop."
6. "Hattie Ranking."
7. Werner and Smith, *Overcoming the Odds*; and Wolin and Wolin, *The Resilient Self*.
8. Tiet, Huizinga, and Byrnes, "Predictors of Resilience."
9. "Just Say No."
10. Turner, "Crack Epidemic."
11. Evans, Garthwaite, and Moore, "White/Black Educational Gap."
12. Tiet, Huizinga, and Byrnes, "Predictors of Resilience."
13. Werner and Smith, *Overcoming the Odds*.
14. "President Nixon Signs Legislation."
15. Tiet, Huizinga, and Byrnes, "Predictors of Resilience"; Werner and Smith, *Overcoming the Odds*; and Wolin and Wolin, *The Resilient Self*.
16. Joyce and Showers, *Student Achievement Through Staff Development*.
17. Carter, *On Purpose*, 143–56.
18. Jones et al., *Navigating SEL*.
19. "Number of High-Poverty Schools Earning."
20. Marzano, *Art and Science of Teaching*.

Resources

Carter, S. *On Purpose: How Great School Cultures Form Strong Character*. Thousand Oaks, CA: Corwin Press, 2011.

Coleman, R., T. Hamrick, J. Hodge, and H. Perkins. *Standing in the Gap: A Guide to Using the SAME Framework to Create Excellent Schools*. Virginia: DreamMakers Publishing, 2004.

Evans, William N., Craig Garthwaite, and Timothy J. Moore. "The White/Black Educational Gap, Stalled Progress, and the Long-Term Consequences of the Emergence of Crack Cocaine Markets." *Review of Economics and Statistics* 98, no. 5 (2016): 832–47.

Hattie, J. *Visible Learning for Teachers: Maximizing Impact on Learning*. New York: Routledge, 2012.

"Hattie Ranking: 252 Influences and Effect Sizes Related to Student Achievement." Visible Learning. https://visible-learning.org/hattie-ranking-influences-effect-sizes-learning-achievement/.

Hess, K. K., B. Jones, D. Carlock, and J. Walkup. "Cognitive Rigor: Blending the Strengths of Bloom's Taxonomy and Webb's Depth of Knowledge to Enhance Classroom-Level Processes," 2009.

Hodge, J. W. "Let Our Youth Speak: A Phenomenological Analysis of Resilience in Students with Multiple Risk Factors." PhD diss., The Virginia Polytechnic and State University, 2009.

Hodge, J. W., and H. W. Perkins. "Louisiana's High Poverty High Performing Schools Initiative: An Executive Summary Developed by Urban Learning and Leadership Center for The Louisiana Department of Education." 2010.

Jones, Stephanie M., et al. *Navigating SEL from the Inside Out*. 2nd ed. Cambridge, MA: The EASEL Lab, Harvard Graduate School of Education, July 2021. https://www.wallacefoundation. org/knowledge-center/Documents/navigating-social-and-emotional-learning-from-the-inside-out-2ed.pdf.

"Just Say No." History, last updated August 21, 2018. history.com/topics/1980s/just-say-no.

Marzano, R. J. *The Art and Science of Teaching: A Comprehensive Framework for Effective Instruction*. Alexandria, VA: Association for Supervision and Curriculum Development, 2007.

National Scientific Council on the Developing Child. "Supportive Relationships and Active Skill-Building Strengthen the Foundations of Resilience: Working Paper No. 13." 2015 https://developingchild.harvard.edu/resources/supportive-relationships-and-active-skill-building-strengthen-the-foundations-of-resilience/.

———. "Young Children Develop in an Environment of Relationships: Working Paper No. 1." 2004. https://developingchild.harvard.edu/resources/wp1/

"Number of High-Poverty Schools Earning High-Performing Distinction Climbs Again." Louisiana Department of Education, January 31, 2011. https://www.louisianabelieves.com/newsroom/news-releases/2011/01/31/number-of-high-poverty-schools-earning-high-performing-distinction-climbs-again.

"President Nixon Signs Legislation Banning Cigarette Ads on TV and Radio." History.com, last updated March 30, 2021. https://www.history.com/this-day-in-history/nixon-signs-legislation-banning-cigarette-ads-on-tv-and-radio.

Stedman, James B. *Goals 2000: Educate America Act Implementation Status and Issues*. Washington, DC: Congressional Research Service, Library of Congress, 1995.

Tiet, Q. Q., D. Huizinga, and H. F. Byrnes. "Predictors of Resilience Among Inner City Youths." *Journal of Child and Family Studies* 19 (2010): 360–78.

Turner, Deonna S. "Crack Epidemic." *Encyclopedia Britannica*. 2017.

https://www.britannica.com/topic/crack-epidemic.

Joyce, Bruce and Showers, Beverly. *Student Achievement Through Staff Development*. ASCD, 2002.

Webb, N. "Depth-of-Knowledge Levels for Four Content Areas." Unpublished paper, March 28, 2002.

Werner, E. E., and R. S. Smith. *Overcoming the Odds: High Risk Children from Birth to Adulthood*. Ithaca, NY: Cornell University Press, 1992.

Wolin, S. J., and R. S. Wolin. *The Resilient Self: How Survivors of Troubled Families Rise Above Adversity*. New York: Vallard Books, 1993.

Acknowledgments

First, I thank my Lord and Savior, Jesus Christ, the major source of my resilience. I thank my wife, Richelle, and her parents, who have been so encouraging and supportive throughout this entire process. My siblings, Tia and Nikki, and their children have been a source of continuous inspiration. I also sincerely appreciate my uncles, Dr. James Fuller and Rev. Dr. Willie T. Ramey, who filled the huge void left in my heart when I lost my father. I thank educators like James Hayden, Donald Humphrey, Lee Vreeland, and others who enhance resilience in kids every single day. I also thank the children of An Achievable Dream who continue to inspire my work. To Richard, Harvey, Shannon, Jerome, and the rest of my family at Urban Learning and Leadership Center, this would not have been possible without you. Finally, I thank Jennifer Deshler and the wonderful folks at NCYI for giving me the opportunity to help others through writing. Thank you for this book and those that will follow. God bless you all.

DOWNLOADABLE RESOURCES

The resources in this book are available
for you as a digital download!

Please visit **youcangetintheway.com** to access the
downloadable resources. Please enter the code below
to unlock the activities.

Please enter code:

GITW436

They may forget your name, but they will never forget how you made them feel.

Maya Angelou

About the Author

Dr. John W. Hodge is president and cofounder of Urban Learning and Leadership Center (ULLC), an organization focused on student achievement and reduction of the achievement gap. Dr. Hodge has over twenty-eight years of experience in education and is a nationally recognized consultant. During his career, Dr. Hodge has provided training and support to educators in over three hundred rural, urban, and suburban school districts that serve over a million students in the United States, Canada, and South America. His work and expertise are particularly focused on the areas of leadership, student achievement, equity, student resilience, poverty, and high academic achievement despite the presence of risk factors.

Dr. Hodge served as a reading teacher, English teacher, AVID (Advancement Via Individual Determination) teacher, and assistant principal of a large urban middle school that received recognition by the United States Department of Education as a National Blue Ribbon School. Following his success in this position, Dr. Hodge was named Associate Director of AVID Center Eastern Division, where he provided training and support to all AVID schools and district support teams in the eastern United States. His passion and enthusiasm for working with underserved student populations resulted in him being named director of An Achievable Dream Academy, a high-poverty inner-city school in the Commonwealth of Virginia. An Achievable Dream served over one thousand K–12 students, over 95 percent of whom lived in poverty. It was here that many of the interventions used by Urban Learning and Leadership Center were piloted. Under the leadership of Dr. Hodge, An Achievable Dream Academy was named a National School of Character and won the Mutual of America Community Partnership Award (MACPA), a national award that annually recognizes organizations that make significant societal impact. Dr. Hodge's leadership, expertise, and collaborative spirit resulted in the academy becoming a fully accredited, high-performing school.

The success of An Achievable Dream Academy became the catalyst for the creation of Urban Learning and Leadership Center. Recognizing the expertise of the ULLC staff and the efficacy of its school improvement model, Governor Mark Warner and Dr. Jo Lynne DeMary, Superintendent of Public Instruction for the state of Virginia, selected the Urban Learning and Leadership Center to provide training for selected schools statewide. This effort was called the Governor's Urban Learning and Leadership Institute. The training institute served as the genesis for the Governor's Partnership for Achieving Successful Schools (PASS) initiative. PASS targeted the state's academically warned schools based on results of Virginia's Standards of Learning exams.

John received his bachelor of science degree from North Carolina A&T State University, where he graduated with honors. He later received his master of arts degree from Chapman University. John completed his academic and professional preparation by earning a doctor of education degree from Virginia Tech, where he conducted extensive research on factors that contribute to the academic success and/or failure of impoverished children.

What sets Dr. John W. Hodge apart in the field of education is his well-documented ability to put research and theory into everyday practice in rural, urban, and suburban schools. Dr. Hodge has helped educators in elementary, middle, and high schools make the necessary changes to help all children meet and exceed rigorous academic standards. He is known as a master teacher and staff developer. Dr. Hodge's career has been defined by assisting students and teachers overcome obstacles and achieve goals. He has also served as an inspirational speaker throughout the United States.

Meetings and Conventions Magazine, a leader in the conventions industry since 1965, polled conference organizers about the best speakers they'd heard in recent years. Poll respondents listed Dr. John Hodge along with Mr. Steve Forbes, Gen. Colin Powell, former First Lady Laura Bush, Dr.

Condoleezza Rice, and Rev. John Maxwell among America's very best speakers. Dr. John W. Hodge is truly one of America's most respected voices in education. His seminars are often "the spark" for schools in their quest to meet and exceed state/federal accreditation standards and implement strategies for continuous improvement. Dr. Hodge is an expert in helping schools create and sustain academic excellence.

Prior to starting his career in education, Dr. Hodge distinguished himself in the service of our country with the 7th Infantry Division of the United States Army.

Be the ONE!

The education of America's youth is a challenging prospect when one considers the many burdens faced by impoverished children and their families. Research indicates that poverty need not be a barrier to academic excellence. As co-author of the book *Standing in the Gap*, Dr. Hodge states, "Across the nation, schools are demonstrating that it can be done: That students can reach high standards, that all children can succeed, that the gap between white and minority students, poor and affluent, can be closed." More often than not, one caring adult can make all the difference in the world. This presentation will encourage all of us to BE THE ONE.

You Can Get In the Way!

Resilience has never been more important than it is **right now** in America's schools and communities, many of which have been ravaged by risk-factors associated with Covid-19. Today and in the near future, schools must be purposeful in their efforts to foster resilience in students and staff. In the book, *You Can Get in the Way*, Dr. Hodge defines resilience in the following way: "Resilience refers to the ability to *avoid, navigate, bounce back from, get through, get over, go around, or survive adversities of all kinds.*" This session is the perfect way to inspire your school district, schools and/or community stakeholders to take action. In this session, Dr. Hodge provides an overview of the book along with very practical solutions to help buffer the risk-factors that traditionally hold kids back. It's the perfect launch for a new school year, or a needed boost during the tough months that follow. After being shared with over 800 educators in a state-wide conference, this session has already been described as "life-changing" by many of those lucky enough to hear it.

The Six-Step Action Plan Process

Throughout the nation, schools are seeking best practices in school improvement to increase student achievement for all students as we meet the demands of NCLB and the newly emerging Common Core National Standards. Successful schools have determined that highly engaging instruction with a standards-aligned curriculum focus, driven by meticulous data analysis, are the keys to success in this high stakes testing environment. The development process for the ULLC school action plan is a six-step model:

    I. Data Capture and Reporting

    II. Data Analysis

    III. Goal/Objective Setting

    IV. Action Step Development

    V. Monitoring and Adjusting

    VI. Communicating the Plan

Following the S.A.M.E. Pathway to Restorative Justice

S.A.M.E. stands for Social, Academic, and Moral Education. It is a holistic approach to creating and sustaining academic excellence in today's schools. S.A.M.E. provides a research supported, holistic view of school improvement by addressing all of the components of school and district culture which must be addressed if lasting school reform is to be attained, i.e. the Social Domain, the Academic Domain and the Moral Domain. As the rigor of state accountability measures increase, schools must focus their efforts to achieve and sustain academic excellence. Come learn how this approach has been particularly successful in schools serving high-poverty populations.

NATIONAL CENTER for YOUTH ISSUES

About NCYI

National Center for Youth Issues provides educational resources, training, and support programs to foster the healthy social, emotional, and physical development of children and youth. Since our founding in 1981, NCYI has established a reputation as one of the country's leading providers of teaching materials and training for counseling and student-support professionals. NCYI helps meet the immediate needs of students throughout the nation by ensuring those who mentor them are well prepared to respond across the developmental spectrum.

Connect With Us Online!

@nationalcenterforyouthissues

@ncyi

@nationalcenterforyouthissues